Anywhere but Benidorm!

A humorous account of Lorraine's life as a part-time expat and her love/hate relationship with all things Spain

Lorraine Carter

Lorraine Carter

Mum & Dad & Ernie for all the love & being there from the start of my journey & for Sheila joining us so soon after.

To my beloved Bob for always being my rock and holding my hand through our many adventures.

To my darling Hayley for the fun, silliness, cake & bubbles & for bringing Sean into our lives. Firmo Love Forever

To My Dear Friend Gary,

Please forgive typos, this is a pre print copy.

thank you for your gift of friendship.

Lorraine xx

Travel makes one modest. You see what a tiny place you occupy in the world.
GUSTAVE FLAUBERT

Contents

Introduction

A broadcaster for many years, Lorraine received an MBE in 1998. She was used to efficiency, precision and speedy exactness in her life. But all that changed when she attended a travel show and took up the offer of a property viewing trip abroad. She had no idea that it would change her life for the foreseeable decade and a half.

On her journey Lorraine almost makes a new home for ITV's Coronation Street, introduces her friend, actress, Sherrie Hewson (*Benidorm's* Joyce Temple Savage) to Japanese food; and declines an invitation to become one of Costa Blanca's new voices on the airwaves. A case of mistaken identity nearly has Lorraine and her husband joining a swingers' group and she finds out about life in Spain as a disabled person when she has a spell in as a wheelchair user.

This is an account of Lorraine's life as a part-time expat and her love/hate relationship with all things Spain.

Preface

My husband, Bob, and I did what many couples did in the heady days of the new millenium and bought a holiday home in the sun, finally finding our dream *casa* in Spain.

For 15 years we led a parallel lifestyle , where the wardrobe contents in one country in no way resembled its sister wardrobe in another.

I hope you enjoy my story of our glimpses into a slower pace of life, and the stresses and strains that only a "si, manana" can bring.

Prologue

Rebecca Foden, born in the slums of Manchester in 1918, hated her name and wanted to be called Mary.

On Bonfire Night 1938, she met Ernest Thompson; for our purposes henceforth known as Big Ernie. They subsequently married and had a son, Ernest William Thompson – again, for our purposes, known as Young Ernie. The second world war was upon them and they, like so many, were literally on the bread line. Rebecca, her son too young to be billeted to the country, at times ran through the streets with bomb shrapnel nipping at her ankles and got home to find the house they had rented was no longer there.

They also longed for a daughter. After the war, they applied for a war refugee but instead they got me, Lorraine Christine, born at home in 1953. I was left to one side in a drawer, a makeshift cot, thought to be dead, as the doctor fought to save Rebecca, who was just about alive; and then, by a miracle, so was the baby.

Young Ernie was delighted to have a sister and at the tender age of 12, he had painted the spare room in sunshine-yellow, ready to welcome his new sibling into her proper cot. The invisible thread wound around their hearts that day and will never be broken.

The early 1950s were gruelling for many and while dad worked 'doublers' at the railway as a labourer, life was tough and not getting any better. They decided to emigrate to Australia.

With an ailing baby, a young son and £30 between them they had little to lose.

The official at Australia House in London took pity on them and added an extra '0' to the declaration, so with £300 on paper only, they sailed on the overcrowded SS Australia by way of the 'Ten Pound Poms' scheme. By the time they reached Port

Said in North East Egypt I was deteriorating, and by the time they reached Sydney the ship's doctor told my parents I wouldn't last the night. I did, just, but once housed in their prefabricated accommodation the following day, my 13-year-old brother and my father braved the torrential rain to walk up the foot of the Blue Mountains to find the doctor whose details they had been given. He duly came and gave me a course of treatment that saved my life but took a huge chunk of our £30.

Dad went to work at the steelworks at Port Kembla where he would complete yet more double shifts to save the cost and time of coming back-and-forth on the single-track railway. Although this worked for a while, he would sometimes be so exhausted he would fall asleep on the train and find himself back where he started, meaning he had to begin the whole journey again.

Young Ernie was sent as an apprentice. How the Aussies loved the thought of a 13-year-old 'English Pom' coming to join them. As it had taken the rest of the meagre £30 to pay for his apprenticeship, my brother was reticent to admit to my parents that he feared for his life. This was no exaggeration as the last apprentice had died when he was put in a water barrel and rolled down a hill. When the 'barrel' test came to my brave brother he survived but realising that he was very quiet and unhappy my mother pressed him for the reason. My parents did not hesitate in forgoing the income and my brother never went back to the job. He did, however, find his own niche, settling with a job in a pie shop. How he would regale us with stories about his boss, the same stories of which have become legend within our family. One of two particular favourites was the day the boss realised he had lost his gold ring in the pies he had been making, so he made my brother stick his finger in every single one until he found the ring; they were then dispatched for sale to the local shop as usual. The other famous story is the time Young Ernie's boss had heard from his divorce solicitor that his long suffering (soon to be ex-) wife, was entitled to half the furniture in the marital home. Without further ado, he set about sawing every piece of it in half.

My parents had bought a trunk for the hold on the SS Australia but sadly, when it reached Mum and Dad, all the contents were ruined, everything had been damaged by sea water, and there was no insurance from which to claim.

Rebecca, frugal as ever, wearing 'galoshes', one pair of the only two pairs of shoes she possessed and brought from England, began saving so they could all return home. Yes, she was homesick, but she also feared that Young Ernie would be called up to fight in the brewing Vietnam war – she had not saved one child from death in Australia just to lose the other one. Big Ernie and Young Ernie would have stayed and made a life in Australia but mother was adamant. Her savings enabled a passage for us all on the SS Orcades – and this time there was no 'third class' for the Thompsons!

Meanwhile, as we sailed the high seas, stopping off for 'Cook's Tours' (at the time a posh excursion tour company) in Cape Town, Ceylon and many other beautiful ports, back in England a 16-year-old beauty called Sheila Phillips went to a local gypsy fortune teller. The mystic told her that the love of her life, a tall, dark, handsome stranger would cross the seas, find her and marry her. She came out of the gypsy's tent thinking that she had 'been done'! Little did she know how true the prophecy was and Young Ernie was just a few nautical miles away. They have now been married for 59 years.

After the first night in the UK, Mum and Dad decided that they had made the wrong decision, that they should have stayed in Australia after all, but they did not have enough money to travel back as they would not be entitled to a further assisted passage. They stayed, bought a terraced house in Manchester, Dad got a job on the railways, as did my brother – but eventually went on to become a police chief.

The seed of wanderlust however had taken its root in their children and sure enough many years later their respective stars would see them travel abroad to have their own holiday homes. This is my story.

Chapter 1

New Beginnings

The beginning of this chapter sees the end of someone else's. Mum had died. After sixty years of married life, my dad working 'all hours God sends' until he died some ten years before, and my mum's scrimping and saving and buying the PG Tips from the supermarket two miles away instead of from the more expensive corner shop; the extra pennies saved had made up my brother Ernie's and my inheritance.

Our dear mum had left us nearly £22,000. She had intended to leave us over £24,000 but solicitors must eat, I suppose!

For years, Mum had recorded the TV programmes showing hopefuls buying a dream in the sun. 'You'll never be able to do that on the pittance I'm going to be able to leave you," joked Mum, "just go and spend it on a blooming good holiday!" My mum told it how it was, bless her.

I wanted a lasting memorial to Mum and Dad's labours for me, as did Ernie. He and Sheila had bought a conservatory for their house with his share, and I was in a quandary. What should I do with mine?

In my role as a radio broadcaster I was fortunate to be invited to many things and one event, in the spring following Mum dying in the January, was to a holiday show in Manchester. While speaking with a gentleman whose stand was all about caravanning in France, I told him politely that caravanning wasn't for me. My husband, Bob, had suggested we give it a try, but I had never wanted to, nor had I any intention of doing so. It was hotels all the way for Bob and me, and we travelled extensively (obviously due to my wanderlust star). The erstwhile salesman threw down the gauntlet by appealing to my frugal side.

"What have you got to lose, apart from a cheap flight and our four-day inspection trip costing £20?" he cajoled.

"Let's stay in a caravan in the South of France!" I announced to Bob when I returned home. Bob didn't need asking twice. He got his maps out – as it very much were – and started planning. Never having been to the South of France, here was the start of a new adventure.

In late spring, we found ourselves driving on the hairpin bends on the way to the caravan park near Pont-du-Loup, a few hair-raising miles from Nice on the Cote d'Azur. We had spent quite a long time in the car park at Nice Airport. My darling 6 ft 2in, lion of a hubby, was sitting on a wall with a Silk Cut cigarette in one hand and the keys to our hire car in the other, too petrified to move or drive! He hadn't told me he was so nervous, and I don't think he knew himself until his nerve stayed somewhere on the cut-price easy-flight from Liverpool. Being the stalwart he is, he screwed his nerve to the sticking place and got on to the *autoroute*, driving like a bat out of hell.

When one is lost in the mountains above Nice it is amazing how fluent one's school-day French becomes. When hope was all but lost, we turned another terrifying bend and – *voila!* A haven? More like Heaven! – caravans, a pool, a well-stocked rustic shop with bread, wine and cheese... *Bonjour, le caravanning!*

We had a lovely weekend and, for a woman who up until then had always said, "I don't *do* caravans", I now did. Except of course, they were not caravans – they were mobile homes!

Still, second-hand caravans – sorry, mobile homes – were £6,000 and soon I got cold feet – and not from the cool air of the Alpes-Maritimes. So, I said to my Bob... "you know love, £6,000 is a lot of money, there are all the service charges and other costs... let's wait a year."

The seasons came and went and true to my word, just before the local Gatley Festival where we lived in Cheshire, we were off again to the cara… sorry, mobile home, site. Bob, now so comfortable with the drive we took last year, had picked up the keys from the car hire desk and was waltzing out happily past the poor pale husbands not daring to sit in their French hire cars – and then stopped dead in his tracks. "Ah yes, I see you are impressed," smiled the young man from the hire car company, "Yes, you have been upgraded!"

Bob swallowed hard. "Oh my God, not a flash car, I'm not that confident," he whispered through clenched teeth as the young man went through the checklist. "OK, let's go, "said Bob. "It's already getting dark and we've got those ravines to negotiate."

The temperature had dropped rapidly as we climbed towards the mountains; from 20°C, it was soon 16°C, then 14°C. We were in t-shirts, our teeth were chattering, my sandaled feet were blue… the problem? We had absolutely no idea how to put the roof up on the beautiful black Opel car!

Following our safe arrival and refreshed from a night's sleep and a good read of the car instructions, we were once again exploring the sky-blue French Riviera. Picnics became de rigueur as we travelled along the coast road, each beauty spot more stunning than the last. Our picnics became much more exotic with each passing day. Years ago, when we were six for a picnic, with our children's ages ranging from seven to 15 years, sandwiches and crisps and fruit were the order of the day. Now, olives and homemade dips, speciality crackers, local cheeses and pâtés were washed down with a modicum of wine – as Bob would not chance a drop over the legal alcohol limit. We had a few small setbacks, such as the day I forgot the corkscrew – however, the cork pushed into the bottle with a biro still tasted like nectar.

Then there was the day we chose a small public beach, just outside La Croisette, Cannes, for our rest-stop, and I realised I had forgotten the plastic wine glasses, so we had no suitable receptacle to imbibe from. We decided we would 'swig' it from the bottle, but realised we needed something to keep the sand off.

So, in a stroke of genius, we used a brown paper bag to hold the bottle.

Right at that moment, three huge 4X4 cars screeched to a halt behind us, parked up, and out spilled an array of children, looking like models from a designer catalogue, with the most gorgeous women. We soon realised they were nannies taking their employers' little darlings for some playtime on the beach. There were some pointed looks (and some actual pointing) and very quickly the children were rounded up, belted back up in their luxurious seats and the super nannies sped off in convoy. It was at that moment we realised that the Gucci nanny brigade had mistaken us for two winos! Now, why would they think that?

The roads leading to our mobile home site, from any direction, meant an exhilarating drive and, once Bob was able to relax a little, the towns and villages around Pont-du-Loup soon enchanted and entranced us. It was easy to see why, during World War II, the activity of those brave members of the resistance movement flourished among the winding medieval streets of Tourettes-sur-Loup, or the cavernous mountains surrounding Grasse. Equally fascinating, but for entirely different reasons, were three concrete edifices guarding the beach and marina of Villeneuve-Loubet, the apartment buildings reminiscent of three latter-day pyramids.

On a day where I had remembered every item of our picnic, we chose the beach of Villeneuve-Loubet to sit and eat our repast. I looked up at the balconied apartments, tiered in a way that each would capture the Riviera sun. I had an idea.

"Darling, we should buy property, not a mobile home!"

Bob, sanguine to my ideas said, "It's a bit more than £6,000, love. How would we do it?"

We began to seek out estate agents' windows when we were in Nice and its environs – although, we didn't bother looking in Monte Carlo. We knew our limits!

We courteously jostled along with all the other upwardly-mobile forty-somethings as we peered at various pictures of apartments, and cottages with lavender gardens. Like our fellow dreamers, we pretended that we understood every word of the *immobilier* listings; although it became quite easy to understand where prices were concerned.

It was obvious that £6,000 converted to euros - even though the exchange rate was good - was still not enough. It was at that point I had my next brainwave. Why not sell our lovely Brooklea – our house in Cheshire which, albeit beautiful, was larger than we needed now our four children had flown, or were flying, the nest.

"You spend every other Saturday mowing half an acre of lawn, while I am dusting and vacuuming huge rooms that are not even used," I reasoned. "Let's sell up and move somewhere smaller and see if we can use Mum's money and some of the money we make from the sale to buy a little place in France?"

Bob enveloped me in a bear hug; I took that as a yes. The last baby would be flying off to university in Paris, no less, in a matter of months, and the world was our oyster!

This was a momentous bolt of lightning for us and within minutes of wanting to buy a mobile home in France with my small inheritance, the next moment we were set to be Francophiles.

We flew home from France, told the kids our plans and set about selling up.

Bob also regaled them with stories of how I cajoled him to drive to Monaco; on the way, he saw a very high outcrop of rock standing majestically out into the sea. "Goodness, I wouldn't like to be the mug who tried to drive up there! "exclaimed Bob. I hadn't told him that 'up there' was Monaco, but he did it, another first! More laughter followed when I, being the navigator, insisted Bob park on a white marked box, in the middle of the blocked-off road in Monte Carlo. I presumed this to be for disabled parking, so we merrily set the clock on my disabled badge, got out and locked up and the realised we were actually on the starting grid of the circuit for the Monaco Grand Prix, which was due to take place the following week!

Meanwhile, back to Gatley. The estate agent's eyes lit up when he saw our property. "A large property of considerable character in half an acre of land in a much sought-after area," the young valuer cooed. "No time at all to sell," he said. We were delighted when he set an asking price considerably higher than we could have dreamed of for our cherished home.

After a few months, we'd had a handful of prospective buyers. Among them we met the family who must have been the inspiration for TV's The Royle Family, as well as the family who nearly forgot to take their Grandma home with them. Not forgetting the man who came to view and asked me, "Eh love, d'you come with the fixtures and fittings?"

Well, we were becoming slightly uneasy. We'll spare you the grim details; however, after lowering the price, we sold. The day after we moved we found we had sold to people who happened to be developers in disguise (but buyer beware – Karma rules, and I later learned their planning application was rejected)

We decided that, as we spent most of our working life in Manchester City Centre, we would purchase a city apartment.

It had been a long winter, so we decided on a short break to Majorca while the conveyance took place. For many years my mum, my daughter Hayley and I had holidayed there, and it seemed fitting to my dear departed mum's memory to go back.

It was also where I went after my divorce and I wanted to show my beloved second husband, Bob, where I rang him from in the early days of our courtship and pre-mobile phones, so I could hear his voice and talk about the time we would be together forever. Now we were together and not only that, we were on the brink of a new second part of our married life, criss-crossing the channel between England and France.

It was time to get our dreams into gear, put our plans in action. Bob had been dedicating half an hour every night to learning French, ready for our holiday home purchase. Everyone knew about our plan to buy our tiny piece of France and we had every French property magazine and book you could think of for Christmas from the family. Bob, ever the chef in our marriage, had onion soup off to a tee and added *Herbes de Provence* to every dish.

As we were sitting watching the sun dance on the waves in Ca'n Pastilla in Majorca, I said to Bob, "Darling, I've been thinking..." (Ever since, Bob has regarded this sentence as a life-changing statement). "You know Spanish prices are much cheaper than France...? It's the same sun, same sea, why don't we buy a holiday home in Spain...?"

Bob's face was a picture. He is not a placid, pushover of a man, and he is a shrewd businessman with a larger-than-life personality. I am fortunate that (mostly) even to this day, he thinks my ideas are good. This time I waited with bated breath.

"So," he said in a measured tone, "After buying 'Living in France', 'Property in France' every other type of book on France; after searching the websites, watching every reality programme on moving to France... After the children bought us Eiffel Tower and Parisian bistro prints... after me playing my 'Learn French in Two Weeks' in the car for the last two years... you want to move to flaming Spain? You now want us to eat tapas and drink cava and learn Spanish and start again on a search of localities?"

Eyes wide, I nodded, awaiting a final answer.

"Brilliant! I was thinking the same!" he cried. Then, very seriously, he looked at me intently - "I have one non-negotiable proviso though. As long as IT'S NOT BENIDORM!"

I was happy to accept his terms, as I was sure I would have the opportunity to visit Benidorm at some point. "Darling,' I nodded fervently, "I wholeheartedly agree, Spain, yes, but let's look for rural Spain."

We sealed our future with a kiss.

"We won't tell anyone yet love," I said. That was easy as my Bob probably thought I would change my mind yet again. So, it was back to the Internet, slyly reading books about Spain, and taking on those scary visits to hotels on Sundays to be plied with cheap Sangria and glossy pictures of smiling fifty-somethings on golf courses.

We quickly became disillusioned. The prices were out of our range and most of the sales persons looked about seven, or seventy, years old, all with an orange perma-tan.

We did however know the area we wanted to look at. We had read that Murcia, south of Alicante in the Costa Blanca, was the up-and-coming area. The airport was being revamped from being a military airport and was due to be enlarged, and the surrounding property was going up fast – both in brick and price. We thought this area was for us and when Bob read that parts of the Dollars Trilogy films were shot (if you'll pardon the pun) not far from there, we knew this was the area for us.

So, one Saturday when sifting through the newspaper adverts, I noticed a property fair was taking place at a restaurant in Manchester. It was in La Tasca on Deansgate, which was beautifully decorated with all things Spanish, complete with loud Spanish guitar music and a bit of wailing thrown in for good measure.

We walked in feeling rather deflated and came face-to-face with a smart fortysomething lady sitting on a barstool. "*Hola!*" she said with a smile. She then chuckled at our reaction. "Don't worry!" she beamed. "I'm Sandra, and I'm originally from Warrington."

Sandra explained over a glass of wine how she and her husband had joined the long line of expats who had bought a holiday home and became so enamoured with Spain that they never came back – except for business.

With that, five weeks later we were on a scheduled flight to Alicante. Bob had got very cold feet in the days preceding our visit. Ever the optimist, I told him, "It'll be fine!" Although deep down, I did worry if the lovely Sandra was a 'front' and we would be locked in a room (or worse) if we didn't 'sign on the dotted line.'

Getting up at 4am for the early flight wasn't so much fun. We touched down at 11am, Bob having nicotine withdrawals and decidedly not a happy bunny. But as we walked out into the sunshine, there was a man awaiting us, holding a big sign with our names on.

"*Hola*, I'm Bill," the man said with a Scottish lilt as he shook our hands and led us to his parked car.

"Hi, I'm Lorraine."

"And I'll sit in the back," mumbled Bob.

We began the long trip to Murcia, around one and half hours from Alicante. Bill drove the long, straight, well-kept roads as he told us how he and his partner, Pete, had settled in an area called Polop de la Marina up the coast.

"OK," said Bill, "so you want to see everything. You have an open mind then?"

"We want to see everything!" we said in unison. Bob had cheered up extensively since he had found Bill was a fellow smoker and that he hadn't immediately started to 'upsell.'

It was hot for the end of April and we were glad to alight from Bill's car when we reached Murcia. We were introduced to Bill's colleague Mike, who was based in the Murcia office. Mike was quite new to Spain and had decided that the only way to prepare for the forthcoming summer's high temperature was to keep his coat on for as long as he could bear it. Since his coat was leather he looked exceedingly hot under the collar!

We had a coffee, transferred to Mike's car and set off into the hills. Yes, I wanted rural but seeing a cement factory in the middle of nowhere did not fill us with joy. A village then appeared on the horizon. All whitewashed building and bougainvillea flowering early in this arid part of Spain. The scene was completed when we spotted old women in black, sitting on chairs by their front doors – real Spain!!

We parked outside a small villa, which had beautiful views over the land – apart from the open septic tank directly across the unadopted road. Mike used his keys to open the door and we felt like one of those couples on the location TV programmes.

I decided early as we walked through the door that the house didn't have a good vibe. Like many Spanish properties, it had small windows to keep out the sun in summer, as well as the extremely cold winter chill. At this point we did not know about the very cold winter nights (no-one mentioned that!)

We followed Mike upstairs and I noticed an old cot with very life-like dolls arranged in it. I had an overwhelming urge to either pull back the curtains and throw open the casement window, or throw up. I couldn't wait to leave and whispered to Bob that I was convinced this dreadful place had once been the local abortion house! We returned to the car in silence, stalwartly looking ahead. I knew Bill and Mike would be able to see any knowing looks in their rear-view mirror and we didn't want to give any outside indication of panic.

Bill and Mike must have sensed our disquiet and took us for an amazing tapas lunch in the neighbouring beautiful town of Lorca. Later, we found out that after centuries of most of the land and water supplies being owned by a minority of landowners and by the church, tourism was growing slowly. Today, its economy is still largely based on agriculture and stock breeding, and there is a large peasant population that come from Ecuador and Morocco.

Little did we know on that hot day in April, that in a few years' time, in 2011, there would be a serious earthquake in Lorca. Lorca is in Murcia and Murcia is therefore close to the large faultline beneath the Mediterranean Sea where the European and African continents meet. While there are many tremors in Spain each year, most are hardly felt. But this one would be the worst in Spain around 4.4 on the Richter scale, killing at least 10 people and injuring hundreds.

Spirits rising once more, we were taken to a 'new build' apartment. "Wait till you hear the crickets," expounded Mike. Well we couldn't hear the crickets; their song must have been drowned under their hard hats. It was an ugly building site! We wrung our hands and apologised that we didn't like it at all. Quite why we apologised I've no idea, but we are British!

"Never mind, better luck tomorrow," Bill encouraged, and we could see he understood our disquiet. He was keen to get us back in his car, waving Mike and his leather coat away as soon as possible.

"Let's get you back to your hotel," said Bill offering Bob a cigarette.

We were relieved – as well as tired, hot and downtrodden.'

"Yep," continued Bill, "You'll both be fine when we get you put up in Albir, it's just around the headland from Benidorm."

"What?!" we cried.

"Oh no, NOT Bloody Benidorm!" exclaimed my Bob.

Chapter 2:

"Not Bloody Benidorm!"

You could have cut the silence with a Spanish Navaja knife as Bob inaudibly seethed in the back of the car. If I had known then that Lorca also produced gun powder, I might have been even more worried he was about to blow a gasket!

I jabbered on as usual, attempting to fill the great divide between Bill in the driving seat and my husband, who I imagined to be in foetal position across the back seat. I thought it might be best to stop speaking in case I said anything that may have prompted Bob to join in. I was worried that if he did, he might use the opportunity to pour forth his pent-up loathing of Benidorm onto poor Bill who was, after all, our chauffeur to the area that Bob had once referred to in conversation as 'a hellish place.'

By now the sun was beginning to dip and I was relieved that Bill had the forethought to use the time to make some hands-free telephone calls. Eventually I began to see what I had been pretending to look out on for the past hour. I couldn't help but gasp at the beauty of the region. I smiled to myself as I saw the larger-than-life silhouette of the legendary black Osborne bull, once used to advertise Osborne brandy but now a symbol of all things Spanish, on a nearby hill. Although I couldn't see him from the front seat, in my mind's eye it adequately represented Bob's mood at that moment. Not that I had ever previously likened him to a raging bull!

I understood his feelings; he had been to Benidorm with another many years before, and it was out of sensitivity to me and testament to the depth of our love that he did not wish to walk on old soil. I was more philosophical and while I didn't have any desire to live in Benidorm, ever since my friend Karl Denver had told me about it, I was curious to visit. I was always happy to see any part of the world that I had not seen before.

Because of our work in the media, we had quite a few celebrity friends, and in fact the first celebrity who tried very hard to encourage me to take my mum and Hayley to Benidorm was Karl Denver, the singer and daddy of the 60s song Wimoweh. For many years I was a producer and presenter with BBC local radio in Manchester, and I was truly honoured to receive an MBE for my work in 2007.

Back in 1991, I was a guest at a charity event and it was on that evening that my then assistant, Colin Owen, and I had an instant rapport with the man singing on stage – although we'd missed his introduction, so we had no idea to whom we were speaking. We all became great friends and Karl supported our charity work almost until his death on 31 December 1998, aged 67.

Karl had told me, in his later years, how he loved performing in the clubs of Benidorm and it was somewhere I had hoped to go to visit and see him perform. Karl, who still had a strong Scottish accent, would say to me, "Come on, take your Mum and the little 'un – they will love it, it's not what you're expecting, there are so many lovely people."

Teddy Bear by Elvis and Karl Denver's Wimoweh are the first two records I remember my brother, Young Ernie, buying and playing on the red gramophone in our living room when I was just six. It was a sore point with my mother as it was the first thing in the family bought 'on tick' (an early buy now, pay later) but I was mesmerised and little did I know that this wonderful singer, Karl Denver, would later become my friend.

Over the years I gleaned more about his past, but I cannot vouch that everything is fact – it is just what I picked up about him along the way. Karl Denver was born Angus McKenzie in Glasgow. Leaving school when he was 15, he joined the Norwegian Merchant Navy and in 1951 he enlisted in the Argyll and Sutherland Highlanders and fought in the Korean war. While he was wounded, he practiced guitar during his convalescence and developed a taste for country and folk music. After being discharged from the army he again went to sea. Music was calling him, and he jumped ship in the United States and made for Nashville, the home of country and western music. Taking the stage name Karl Denver, he appeared on radio and television, and the prestigious Grand Ole Opry show, before the immigration department caught up with him and he was deported in 1959!

Settling in Manchester, he teamed up with Gerry Cottrell and Kevin Neill to form the Karl Denver Trio. They toured the Northern clubs and appeared on Granada Television's Band Stand. In 1961 the trio was 'discovered' by impresario Jack Good, who presented them on his television series Wham! and got them on to a national tour headed by Jess Conrad and Billy Fury. Karl had found his USP, appealing to the music lovers of the sound of the yodelling cowboys exemplified in the 1950s by Slim Whitman, whose signature tune, Indian Love Call, was part of the Denver stage act. Karl himself was hailed in the New Musical Express as 'an artist with a totally different and distinctive approach'. Karl's hits included a pre-1914 Victor Schertzinger song Marcheta, an equally antique French song, A Little Love A Little Kiss, the hillbilly tune Mexicali Rose and Wimoweh.

Karl used to tell me that he discovered the song in South Africa during his days as a seaman but later I read it had already been a hit in the hands of American folk group The Weavers, and The Tokens had re-recorded it with new lyrics as The Lion Sleeps Tonight.

During all these varying accounts, all I do know is that Karl had taken the indigenous people of South Africa to his heart as he would often, over a cup of coffee in my kitchen, reminisce about his time there and the wonderful people he had met. The Karl Denver Trio version displayed Denver's vocal talents and soon they were catapulted to full effect into the upper reaches of British show business. In 1963 the Trio were given their own Light Programme show on the BBC, Side by Side. Among their guests were The Beatles.

Although the Karl Denver Trio faded from the media lime-light, they continued to perform in cabaret at home and overseas, including Karl's favourite… Benidorm. There was a brief, unexpected return to the charts in 1989 when the Happy Mondays had them guesting on their track Lazyitis and on an updated recording of Wimoweh on the fashionable Factory label.

Other celebrity friends had told us about their public appearances in a place called Benidorm Palace, a Las Vegas-style cabaret venue… "Yeah, right," we thought… Oh! How we would eat our words one day!

I had smiled benignly while friends adoringly eulogised the town. As an admitted snob, I had thought of Benidorm as not quite my cup of latte, really.

"There's my mountain!" exclaimed Bill, as he interrupted my reverie - and I was so glad he had. There were the beautiful etched mountains, one of them more pointed than the rest, with an increasingly twinkling curtain of stars and, to the right, rolling hills down to the headland, the sun now threatening to take its orange hue to other continents.

"Darling, darling." I unceremoniously shook Bob, awakening him from what I knew was a pretend slumber. I could feel the tension around him dispel as he looked out in awe, sat up and, in a much friendlier tone, offered Bill a cigarette.

"Where's this then, Bill?" enquired Bob, taking a drag of his low tar cigarette.

Bill, relieved, and glad to be spoken to, pointed to the right. "Any second now and we'll see Benidorm down there. We call it Spanish Manhattan though."

Next minute, there it was. Not bad, not bad at all!

It was 9pm when our Scottish guide swept into a picturesque small town called Albir. Bob was missing his evening tipple of brandy and Coke, and Bill no doubt dreading the thought of another two days in our company, obliged by finding a supermarket. After all, if Bob became Mr Nice instead of Mr Grumpy, Mr Bob would be a better companion for us both!

The silver lining didn't last as the *supermercado* doors were closed in our faces. Oh no. The colour drained from Bill's face under his suntan and we walked, dejected, back to his 4X4. Bill was now caught somewhere between the devil and the sapphire Mediterranean Sea; on the one side his unhappy clients, and on the other his equally unhappy partner, waiting for him at home. Bill's partner, Pete, had called several times and we could now hear his voice becoming louder and more strained through Bill's mobile, so much so that he needed to hold the phone away from his ear. Our faces were no more encouraging, having just been rejected from the only supermarket in the town.

"No worries," said Bill (he said that a lot), as he stoically pressed the key lock to open his car and drove on until he found an open supermarket.

Bob was happy, Bill was happy, Pete would soon be happy. I was plain exhausted.

We were checked in to our complimentary hotel, amusingly called 'Roberto's' – Bob didn't quite get the joke!

Bill made his exit from us very quickly, stepping backwards as he shook Bob's hand and called out, "See you guys at 9am!"

"Let's make it 10," responded Bob.

"No worries!" trilled the disappearing Bill, who would very soon be sharing a bottle or two of Rioja with the long-suffering and very hungry Pete, while he no doubt regaled him with the day's exploits.

If Bill breathed a sigh of relief, so did we. We needed some time together to regroup and discuss, and I needed the toilet!

We had been secretly impressed by the reception area of the hotel and even more so with our room. I emerged from the marble bathroom having completed the necessary and performed a stocktake of the bath soaps and shower gels and other bits and pieces.

I heard Bob call me from the balcony, the view even in the darkness was breath-taking. There was the usual swimming pool, still shimmering blue thanks to the turquoise tiles and flood-lights. Then there was a very realistic lagoon and behind were the mountains of Sierra de Serrella, where car headlights gave the illusion of floating ribbons around the black imposing mountains.

"Now this is more like it," sighed Bob. Oh good, I thought, a breakthrough… sadly, it was to be a short respite as Bob turned to me, his back leaning on the balcony wall, arms folded and a furrowed brow. "But what are we doing so close to Bloody Benidorm? Why did we have to endure two hours' drive back up the coast from the area we specifically told them we wanted to see, and then deposited in a hotel around the headland from Bloody Benidorm?"

Usually, or at least most of the time, I am the voice of reason, the annoying person who finds a silver lining in the darkest cloud. Quite often, people no doubt want to slap me for my optimism and the way I carry around a glass that is always over half full – and that hardly ever spills!

"But we didn't like Murcia, did we?" I reasoned while changing into some cooler trousers. (As an aside, why is that whenever we carefully pack trousers, one leg always seems to work its way inside out, meaning a little one-legged dance must be performed while you waggle your foot into the offending trouser leg?)

I was very hungry, and I was trying to instil a bit of urgency into Bob so that he would get a move on, as it was nearly 11pm. I also thought that should we find that all the local restaurants had already closed in what was still early season, this would do nothing for Bob's spirits, never mind his stomach.

"That's not the point," continued Bob as he held a pair of green chinos in his hand. "THEY didn't know we wouldn't like it, did they, so we shouldn't be in Bloody Benidorm!"

He did have a very good point. I think I had a sneaking suspicion why we had ended up where we were, but then I have always been a fatalist. The area we were in, from what I had seen already, was looking more like the Riviera than the 1960s playground of the pale skinned Brits, the mecca they called Benidorm and Bob had once called 'Hell.'

"Let's go and eat and see what tomorrow brings, love," I encouraged as I took Bob's hairbrush from his hand and replaced it with my hand.

As we walked into 'town' Bob stopped, "You are right, you know. We don't need to buy anything. We are in Spain, we are together, it's a lovely hotel. And I love you very much!"

"I love you too, husband," I whispered as I stood on my tip toes to plant a kiss on his nose.

"Oh God, I've just had a thought," said Bob. "I bet they'll lock us in a room tomorrow until we sign up like those timeshare people do!"

With the last bit of energy I could muster, I squeezed Bob's hand. "Come on love, let's eat!!"

Chapter 3

We had a plan!

The next morning, having awoken to a cold, dark hotel room, we were delighted to throw back the heavy black-out curtains to reveal the sunniest Saturday we had encountered in a very long time.

As we returned from breakfast, the telephone in our room was ringing. We purposefully ignored it as we thought we would be a little wicked and for a few mischievous moments it would allow Bill to think we had 'done a runner.'

Bill was, reassuringly, his cheery self once more and we couldn't help greeting him warmly too. Since our master plan now was that we would not buy any property on this trip, why not be friendly?

Bill led us over to the brown leather sofa in reception. It felt cold on our white legs in our three-quarter trousers. Even though the sun was already high in the Spanish sky, the hotel was dark and cooling, a must for the unrelenting summer to come. The locals who passed through the hotel on business were in dark suits and some with scarves. They would need to be surgically removed, I mused, at least until the temperature rose much higher in the coming months.

Bill, an ex-IT consultant, had set up not one but two laptops on the coffee table in front of us. Perhaps he had stayed all night in reception just in case we had made for home during the early hours.

I did wonder if perhaps ex-IT consultants didn't die, they just moved to Spain to become estate agents.

He had some off-plan new builds to show us and they did look very good even if they weren't yet built. Yes, we were prepared to stand on the hill where the digging would soon start. Yes, we would drive to Denia tomorrow to see an apartment. We had no idea where Denia was, but hey, now we were just on a free holiday, who cared, we would get a free lunch thrown in, too!

Now that we had decided to follow our plan of just smiling and being ready to see anything, life was much easier for us. Bill, on the other hand, was looking slightly uneasy. I could just imagine his mind working overtime – *'Has Bob swallowed a happy pill this morning? Are they both on something? Were they visited during the night by the three ghosts of Christmas?'*

Either way, Bob not being grumpy and me not being jumpy was obviously unsettling.

Just as Bill closed up his mobile office and zipped up his beloved laptops in to their leather cases his mobile rang, right on cue.

Beaming, Bill passed the phone to me. "It's for yoo-hoo," he chimed.

I knew it would be Sandra, the lovely lady we had met back in cold and dark January, her voice was as sunny as ever. She wouldn't take no for answer, we absolutely *must* come to a barbecue at her mountainside villa that afternoon. Transport was no problem as Bill was invited too. I said that would be lovely, and secretly thought it would work well for everyone – Bob and I wouldn't need to be shown any more properties that day, and it also meant that poor Bill received a break from us.

And then, in spite of myself, a slight paranoia crept in, but I was reluctant to share it with Bob. What if that was it? What if we weren't going to Sandra's house at all, but a big barn in the mountains where prospective pale-faced buyers who thought they were on free holiday were locked in until they signed deeds, and we were the final two needed… No, I decided, it would be fine!

Bill's voice jolted me out of my reverie.

"Just before we get gone…. I don't know how you will feel about this, but there is one place that came on the market last night. I don't even have any details for it. It is double the price you had in mind, but as I told you yesterday you won't get anything but a garage with that. I have to go up sometime and pick up the key; do you guys want to come?"

Bob and I looked at each other, and both smiled and shrugged our shoulders at the same time. Now we were co-conspirators in our master plan of not buying, it wasn't like the day before in merciless Murcia, where it all still mattered.

"Why not!" said Bob. I am sure I saw Bill shift uneasily. We were definitely scaring him now we'd become so agreeable.

"Ok then, no worries. Let's go!" said Bill, regaining his composure and clapping his hands on his knees as he stood.

I once more climbed into the front of the car and Bob stepped into the back. We were prepared for the day in more ways than one. After having experienced the long journeys of the day before, without a break, I had brought my bottle of water and Bob had made a mix of brandy and Coke. I realised that Bob must have softened slightly towards Bill, as I noticed he'd brought both the tumblers from the hotel room so he could share his stash. I'm always suspicious that they provide those glasses for guests to soak their false teeth in, so I knew the second glass wasn't intended for me!

We travelled a little way out from Albir and I giggled as we drove through a town called Alfas Del Pi. With my weak bladder I should be the Mayoress, I thought. We chatted about Bill's evening, some of which had been salvaged. Bill had reached the little restaurant in the hills, where he met up with his beloved Pete and his friends. The promised feast had been fabulous but sadly Bill had only managed to arrive in time for the coffee and brandy, but, "Hey, no worries!" chirped Bill. He spoke fondly of the friends he and Pete had made in the relatively short time that they had been there. He spoke of his 'drama queen' mate Joseph, who was one of those Marmite people you loved instantly, or disliked intensely. He spoke of his other friends who loved to do quiz nights but always lost. "When you meet them in the future, you'll see what I mean about Joseph," laughed Bill.

This provoked another furtive glance and subtle guffaw from Bob and me, Bill talking in the future tense and in the assumptive. Oh dear… our plan to look interested was obviously working too well!

We had both separately rationalised that we would most likely return, for a holiday, to this area. It was extremely pretty and nothing like 'Bloody Benidorm.' And we would like to see Bill again and to meet Pete, too.

The road had taken us across a white wrought-iron bridge and then left towards a group of yellow and cream houses in neat rows, nestled in the folds of one of the biggest mountains we had ever seen. Bill swung the car left and stopped on a narrow road.

"This is a nice estate, Bill," I smiled.

"This is *not* an estate - it is an *urbanisation,* my dear," reprimanded Bill.

"Ok then, an urbanisation. Where to now then?" I asked, ever in anticipation of 'the next'.

"Here," said Bill pointing to a house. "The house – or should I say, *casa,* which is just coming onto the market!"

I remember the moment I first met Bob. He had telephoned me to ask if he could be interviewed on my radio programme. He had such a lovely manner and appeared very enthusiastic about his work in the community and was out to convince me how it would be a good idea for the radio station and his organisation to work together. I did detect a slight sales patter in that conversation and I decided I would, as I always had done with pushy interviewees, make him wait a few weeks before inviting him onto the show. It was lucky for both of us that a guest had cancelled at the last minute, so I allowed Bob to think he had performed a marvellous selling job on me and I, in return, filled my empty programme slot with an articulate person.

He was the last guest on my live show. It was the very early nineties and as I looked through the studio glass window into the control room, I saw a handsome man, in a white shirt, grey tie and black suit. He had premature grey hair, but it was thick and wavy, what my mother would call 'a good head of hair.' I smiled and waved as I always did to my guests, and he waved back with his left hand. I sighed in trepidation as I saw the large wad of papers he was holding under his right arm. '*Oh no,*' I thought, '*I hope he knows he only has three minutes and then it's the 7pm news.*'

As I closed my penultimate interview, the last victim was ushered out and Bob was unceremoniously pushed into the hot seat by my assistant. After all, she only had twenty seconds to perform the egress and ingress to the studio while a radio jingle was being played.

I smiled at Bob and noticed his gleaming white teeth, and then the red light was on and I was in interview mode, introducing him, live on air to my listeners.

Bob proceeded to rustle through his papers. Anyone who has been in a radio interview situation will be aware that the slightest noise is amplified to the ear of the radio audience. So, with a smile in my voice over the airwaves of Manchester, I glared at Bob as he gesticulated and waved his notes around. In true broadcaster fashion (or perhaps not), I leaned across the desk and I swiped his papers away from him, letting them flutter quietly to the floor. He later said of me that he thought that I was attractive in my short denim skirt and jacket but that I appeared 'very bossy'! The interview went well, and after we came off air we chatted for a short time as we discussed social action matters and he wasted no time in suggesting a competition that could be launched on my programme. I liked him immediately and we became business friends for a long time before each of us became aware that we had been deluding ourselves, and that something had happened to our emotions at a much deeper level. So, had it been love at first sight? We both remember that first glance at each other as being a very special moment.

Another special moment happened that day in Spain in 2004. We both still remember our first glance at this cream and yellow villa as it stood almost expectantly in the sunshine, like a pup in a dog shelter saying, "Choose me, choose me."

How did I feel at that moment? How did my Bob feel? We both felt the same electricity, the same knowing and the same feeling of 'coming home.'

Bill ushered us towards some steps at the side of the house. My heart sank. I wondered if it was in fact an apartment, not a house. But as we climbed then emerged onto a huge sun terrace, known as the solarium, we felt like we were on-board ship, faced with a beautiful pointed mountain before us. It had one big jagged rock missing near its apex, the Puig Campana. The scent of the pine trees was truly overwhelming. We turned 180 degrees and could see the coast and the sea; to our left, another range, the Sierra Bernia, and to our right, yet another. It was part of an urbanisation, but we were on top of the world. We later learned that where the big piece of mountain was missing, folklore told that a giant kicked the mountain and the piece hurtled out to sea and became the island seen from Benidorm beaches.

"What d'ya think?" whispered Bob.

"I love it," I croaked, filled with emotion and a tear escaping behind my sunglasses.

Bob put his arm around me and held me very tightly. For both of us, it was love at first sight.

Bill broke the moment. "Are you two alright up there?"

We straightened and became very jolly once more. "Lovely view!" we shouted in unison as we heard Bill's sandaled feet coming up the terracotta tiled steps.

"Hey, look Bill," said Bob. "The neighbours across the way have got the biggest satellite dish I have ever seen. Bet it's even bigger than yours!" Bill had been telling us, with great pride, that he had a satellite dish in his garden and all his neighbours hooked up to it for their broadband use.

"That *is* my satellite dish!" smirked Bill. "If you were to purchase this highly desirable property, we would be neighbours!"

There are moments in life when one is too stunned to answer and only laughter will fill the space. We hadn't even seen inside the house, we couldn't even remember how much it was on the market for, yet there we were, the three of us, silently knowing that we were going to be neighbours.

Still laughing, we headed down the biscuit coloured steps back to the front door that Bill had unlocked for us. As we entered, he was quick to run around the house and open the shuttered windows, the light pouring into the small abode.

We had just sold our 1930s home in England with its four master bedrooms, its utility rooms, reception rooms and set in half an acre; this Spanish *casa* seemed tiny to us. We had just downsized to a stylish two bedroomed apartment in Salford Quays. Little did we know that years later, having experienced apartment living, we would love 'small', and would in fact find this type of dwelling more spacious than necessary and would long for an apartment abroad, not a house.

But back to the moment. While Bill showed Bob the 'American kitchen' – estate agent speak for 'your lounge and kitchen, separated by a breakfast bar', I poked around the house alone. Good, the bathroom had a bath. Two good sized bedrooms, but I wasn't at all keen on the Ikea look in this setting. For our apartment in England, we had taken the minimalist look, which was ideal where we were. Here in rustic Spain, I couldn't understand why anyone would incorporate Scandinavian décor. I wanted black wrought iron to match the gates, burnt orange, Spanish woods. I realised the two men were laughing at me indulgently. Bill still refrained from asking 'the big question.'

"OK, shall we go?" asked Bill, jangling the keys and closing the shutters making it impossible to see anything in the house we now so desperately wanted. We reluctantly made to leave. Soon we were back out in the blinding sunshine once more, and Bob and I made our way to Bill's car.

"Hey, don't you want to see the pool then?" called Bill over his shoulder, walking to the end of the road. The house we had just seen had enough outdoor space to have a pool installed and it would still have had plenty of room, but we had decided we didn't want the bother of maintaining one. Actually, that was in the same conversation when it was decided we were not going to be sold to!

As we followed Bill and walked a stone's throw away from the house, Bill unlocked some tall iron gates.

They say when you die and go to heaven that the colours are more vivid than real life. Well, perhaps we had passed away somewhere between leaving the house and these non-pearly gates. The crystal water of the swimming pool reflected the azure blue, April sky, the backdrop of the mountain, its paint box palate of green and brown completing the picture.

"Let's get going then," said Bill in the imperative as we jumped back into the now.

As we climbed back into the car, Bill talked about this and that family on the urbanisation, but neither of us were listening, Bob and I united in a stunned silence. Eventually, the inevitable 'Big Question' came from Bill.

"Well?"

"We want it!" exclaimed Bob, so quickly that he made me jump as he leaned forward from the back of the car and tapped me on the shoulder. "We do want it, don't we love?"

"Yes, oh yes!" I squealed and nodded and nodded.

"OK," replied Bill in a level tone, "but I insist you should see other properties this morning."

"Yes Bill," we replied in unison. Our heads were spinning. Solicitor, Spanish mortgage, we can't speak the language, two and a half days till we fly home – and one of those days is a Sunday!

Bill drove us to various areas, where he held paper work and plans up to us, showing where the new builds would be. He asked us to envisage property on them. We nodded along but took in nothing as our minds were too deep in thought. We were glad to eventually head out of the area, climbing and twisting and turning along the hairpin bends of the mountains.

We were due to be in the hills of Pego by 4pm to attend Sandra's barbeque. Each vista was more breath-taking than the last and after what seemed like a total overload of the senses, we reached a tiny village and stopped outside a farmer's market hall. This looked nothing like the market hall my Uncle Len used to work at in Hyde in the North of England. He always said that the only way he would be warm was when he was in the incinerator at the crematorium… we had always been a jolly family! He said the cold and damp had seeped into his bones and the dampness was locked into them. As I turned to admire this one, I hoped that Uncle Len was comfy in a lovely warm farmers' market, like this one, but in the sky.

The sun was now lower, and the hustle and bustle of the day's trade had long since passed. Most likely, the men had been propping up the bar for a few hours now, putting the world to rights. In fact, as I looked at them more closely, I mused that they looked like they may have been there much longer than just a few hours – they looked like they were part of a sepia photograph showing rustic Spain! I had glanced at such scenes in Sunday supplements, the scenes that in truth you hardly ever see on your average holiday.

The market hall was obviously the centre of the community; market in the morning, nursery mid-morning, concert hall come the evening, and most likely wedding venue (although worth bearing in mind that the men at the bar probably come as part of the fixtures and fittings). The high beams gave the place an almost hallowed feel and the exquisite Spanish tiling gave it a museum-like quality. It certainly beat our English pre-fab community centres!

As usual, I needed to use the facilities. Bill pointed to a door and warned me not to expect too much. I entered a tiny room from which I expected a pig or a goat to run out. It was clean though, with a high cistern and a piece of rope hanging down. I wondered how the Spanish ladies reached it as they generally seemed quite short, albeit considerably wider than me. I decided it was best not to dwell on it as the door I tried to close had a four-inch-wide gap. *'No worries,'* I thought, mentally coining Bill's favourite phrase. I just covered the gap with my cardigan and bag as best I could.

When I came out I was met by a lovely scene. Bob was surrounded by these non-English speaking locals who were in the process of giving Bob their wealth of experience on how best to order a glass of white wine and two white coffees. Bill, ever the psychologist, had nipped out to the car, meaning Bob had no choice but to endeavour to communicate with the men and it worked. The drinks were ordered and purchased with much happy gesticulation, back slapping and a supply of Bob's cigarettes!

We took our drinks outside into the little communal terrace with its red tin tables and umbrellas advertising Mahou Beer, pronounced 'Mow'. Fairy lights were strung from umbrella to umbrella and bits of washing were pegged on to the rope between the light bulbs.

It was time for a serious talk. Bill leaned forward, as he stubbed out his cigarette in the red matching Mahou ashtray.

"OK – you definitely, definitely want the property you saw this morning?"

We both nodded at him emphatically.

"Right then, all I need to do is to get the property on the books so you can buy it!"

With that, he pushed his chair back, popped his cigarettes and lighter into his shorts pockets and went to walk out of the market hall.

"What on earth do you mean?" Bob screeched after him in disbelief.

"No worries – we've got two days and counting, you will be in it in three weeks. This is Spain! *Mañana!* Chill out!"

We were certainly chilled. We were frozen with fear. Panic rose, even in my usually calm solar plexus, as we drove once more up through the mountains.

"Bill, it's Saturday afternoon, everywhere is shut on Sundays, even we know that, we fly home tea-time Monday…"

Bill lifted both hands off the wheel in a calming gesture. I hated it when he did that.

"Guys, calm down, just a matter of getting the place on our books, getting you registered in Spain, finding you a solicitor, finding you a bank and getting you a mortgage. No worries."

As I found myself seated by Sandra's pool, looking out at a sea of endless mountain ranges, perhaps it had all been a dream. We were being feted as the new purchasers of a house in Spain, and with the heady mixture of cava and SPF20, suddenly, at that moment, everything and anything seemed possible. After all, as Louis Pasteur said, 'A bottle of wine contains more philosophy than all the books in the world.'

By early evening Bill had dropped us back at our hotel. The April evening had cooled, and Bob and I decided to take a stroll by the sea. The small, modern resort of Albir can be found about 50 minutes' drive North along the motorway from Alicante.

Unlike many other Costa Blanca towns, Albir has been carefully and beautifully planned virtually from scratch. Only one or two of the buildings are over five storeys high, its avenues are broad and tree-lined, with a gorgeous beachside promenade almost 600 metres in length. As dusk turned the sky to ink, we noticed that the amazing beach was for the main part encrusted with white pebbles. These pristine little gems must have saved Albir from the hordes of Benidorm tourists who were at that moment, no doubt, heading in their throngs to the bright lights and delights of Benidorm which nestled just around the headland, with its almost 600 metres of clean, safe, sandy beach.

Our noses were led by the delicious aromas which emanated from a nearby restaurant and we settled in, about to work out our finances. The restaurateur, a man of Egyptian origin, obviously knew the signs as along with the menu he brought out a pad and calculator and as he scraped the legs of the metal chair along the uneven stone floor of his terrace and sat down beside us.

"Good, you have pens, but don't use that scrap of paper! Use this writing pad. Now choose something quickly – you eat, and then we'll talk."

It was happening again; two people who were leaders in their chosen professions, Bob in business and I in the media, were being guided along a path by people who knew more than us, wanted to help us and wanted to do it immediately.

We chose some tapas and wine and sure enough by the time we had mopped up the last of the divine sauce from the terracotta dishes with the last of our bread, he was at the table with a big candle to shed light on our new life. He threw down a ring binder file full of papers, and we talked into the night about the best way to transfer money and which company to use, not to just rely on our banks to transfer. How we would need to put a holding fee of around £2,000 before we left the country. How we would need a *gestor* - a cross between a bookkeeper and a solicitor – and so it went on. It was only when we waved *adios* to our Good Samaritan that we realised we didn't even know his name!

We sauntered back to the hotel. It had become chilly and we could hear the roar of the sea, not even realising it was just around the corner from our hotel, so we went to greet it. Bob put his linen jacket around my shoulders as we stood looking at the white pebble beach being washed by the midnight blue Mediterranean Sea, the moon casting a silvery walkway along the waters. This was the beginning of our new path, a new chapter in our lives.

We had brought up four children between us; even though none of the children were created by our union, we couldn't love each of them more. The villa was the child we had never had together. Today had been the thin blue line on the property pregnancy test – it was real, it was happening and there was no manual for it. And if we did find a manual it would be in blooming Spanish!

Not for one moment now did we regret the consummation of our dreams when we had looked out from that roof terrace only that morning. What a day it had been. We had started the day with a plan not to buy, and look how things can change so quickly. We made for our bed, as property speculators.

We awoke to a Sunday in an out-of-season Spanish town, and what a Catholic Sunday it was. The place was like the Marie Celeste apart from the bells which tolled Mass. That day we were expecting a different kind of baptism, a baptism of fire. Bill was going to take us to Benidorm!

When Bill picked us up on what was only our third day in his company, you would have thought we had known each other for years. Gone was Bob's grumpiness and my nervousness, and in place of it our thanks for him giving up his Sunday to take us to the B-place.

"No, don't be sorry", he said, as he put an arm around my shoulder. "I am supposed to be with you 24/7 so that you don't have the opportunity to change your mind. You've not signed anything yet!"

We promised not to change our minds if he left us in the old town of Benidorm and he could come and pick us up later in the afternoon.

"OK, see that sign there, Sex Shop? I'll meet you by that at 4pm," he shouted from the car window as he turned on a sixpence and sped off to have breakfast with long suffering Pete. Many years later we would enter the doorway beneath the Sex Shop sign to have lunch with a very different sort of lady, a true lady, in her 80s who lived in the same block.

As we turned and walked down the cobbled streets we were met by the sight of a piece of real Spain, which couldn't have been further the Benidorm we had envisaged. We took in the vibrant scene of the stand-up tapas bars, so close together you couldn't tell when one hostelry ended, and another began. The chatter was a mixture of Spanish and Valencian language – not a tourist-orientated venue, a true slice of Spain. We were on Calle Santa Domingo, known in English as 'Tapas Alley.' We continued through the archway and there was a slick promontory, reminiscent of Monte Carlo. It seemed that this weekend was challenging our perceptions of everything. We dropped ourselves into the seats of a wine bar, too stunned to walk any further. In true Victor Meldrew fashion, Bob uttered those immortal words, "I don't believe it!"

I rang Young Ernie from my mobile; he and his wife, our dear Sheila, are both older than us and were both also keen to escape the British winter snows for warmer climes.

"Hi love... Yes, yes we're fine... Yes, we are keeping our passports in the hotel safe... no we are not drinking the tap water... have we done anything exciting? Well yes actually... we've bought a house! It's just outside Benidorm and it's gorgeous..."

My brother doesn't shout but suddenly there was an assault on my ears.

"You've done what?! Have taken leave of your senses?! Not Bloody Benidorm!!"

Usually, the day you are about to travel home from abroad is one for resting, soaking up the last few rays of the sun, and experiencing the last vestiges of the area. This was not to be our itinerary. We needed to be registered in the country, we needed a mortgage and we needed to pay a deposit on the house. Then we needed to check in at the airport.

We were jittering wrecks by the time Bill came to pick us up, early! He of course was his usual unruffled, happy-go-lucky self.

"OK, no worries. I've already checked you out of the hotel, we'll just make the hour's trip into the mountains to my boss's office to get you signed up then we'll start the process."

"No stress there then," I mused.

One hour and several hair pin bends later, we were in the estate agent's office. We met the owner, who reminded me of the Walt Disney character, Cruella Deville, and for a little while I felt like one of those little Dalmatian puppies under her steely gaze. Bill, being of such a sunny nature, must have driven her to distraction!

Cruella shook hands with us and I discreetly wiped my hand on the back of my cotton dress – it was like shaking hands with a corpse. I was feeling very sick from the journey and Bill immediately produced a cup of peppermint tea to revive me. Perhaps all their clients felt like I did before signing!

Luckily, she soon slithered away into her office and the

lovely Sandra appeared through another door. Gone was her sunny yellow t-shirt and shorts and she was dressed in her black Windsmoor suit, looking every inch the professional. The preliminary contract was put before us and we marvelled how, at a press of a button, the contract was translated from Spanish to English. The vendor wanted completion within three weeks; we asked if we could be given until at least the end of May to complete, even though it was the end of April. We didn't receive a verbal response, Bill and Sandra having been in Spain long enough to copy the Spanish way of simply answering with a shrug of the shoulders.

We pressed the point, until the inventory of white kitchen goods (a must in Spain) and the request for a later completion date was added to the contract. As this was being completed, I signed a Visa slip for 2,000 euros as the holding fee on our house. We had effectively just bought a house on Visa!

Sandra hurriedly bustled Bill and us out of the door.

"Go and get their photos done, they aren't registered yet and its nearing Siesta!"

So, Bill, Bob and I were despatched to a nearby village to have our passport-type photos taken.

"No photo booths then, Bill?" I enquired.

With a sigh, Bill answered, "We don't have a Tesco in the village Lorraine, it's Spain!"

Well, silly me – here I was thinking of all the passport/driving licence pictures I had had taken, sitting in a little cubicle with a curtain across with people passing while I tried to adjust the height of the revolving seat, insert my money into the correct place and then tried to relax! No-one's photos ever come out like those of the perfect model plastered to the side of the booth, and we've just become programmed to accept the unattractive version of ourselves contained within five little sticky pictures.

But no, this was a tiny in-land village in Spain, where all such photos are taken at the local photographers. We stepped into, at Bill's behest, a small shop in the middle of a narrow, cobbled street. At first I saw nothing, so bright was the sunshine outside and so cool and dark was the shop. As our eyes became accustomed to the light, we were ushered into a back room and I was first to be seated on a comfortable chair, my head guided this way a little, chin down a little, light adjusted behind me. The photographer pulled a face at the first shot she took of me and then smiled and nodded at the second. Bob, ever photogenic, was up next and in no time at all we were each presented with a beautiful tiny folder with two pictures inside – and what's more, the photos looked like us. What a miracle!

"*Cinco euros, por favor.*" Five euros! Cheap at double the price!

For a moment, lost in the euphoria of our pictures, we forgot we were on a mission.

"No dilly-dallying!" called Bill, as he hot-footed back down the sloping and winding cobble street. "It's off to Denia with you now to the Police station."

We had been to Denia two days before when we were shown around an apartment belonging to a couple who were desperate to move back to England. The block of flats was a mixture of inner-city Manchester and Colditz Castle by the sea. We couldn't wait to leave. Apart from watching the ferry leave from there to take trippers to Ibiza, it held no interest to us at all – but it was now vital to our quest that we return. Bill managed to find a parking space across the busy road from the Police station. I couldn't see a door leading into the official-looking building.

"How do we get in, Bill?" I asked.

"I have no idea," came the reply.

Even Bill was looking worried.

"I have never done this before," he confessed, "and its ten minutes to Siesta time, so it's now or never. RUN!"

We tripped over ourselves, into an office which looked like a 1950s Post Office with a further office beyond. We took a ticket from the wall and stood in a long queue; we had gleaned that when your number was called, you had to hurl yourself into the next room and if you weren't quick, as one lady wasn't, distracted as her child needed to blow its nose, the next number would be called and your chance was gone. We gave only a fleeting, sympathetic look to the crying woman who was told to leave and come back tomorrow.

Ping! Number 23 lit up. Bill pushed us through the threshold and we stood looking at the policeman up on his high chair like we were naughty school children. Bill said something in Spanish, handed over our passports and picture folders, and after much erratic stamping with the official's rubber stamp we were handed a piece of paper each with a gesture which meant, "move a long please" – or more likely, "go on you Brits, get lost!"

Bill took the small pieces of paper from us and explained that he would come back in two weeks with these receipts and pick our NIE papers up for us. We later realised that the NIE papers, the *Numero de Identidad de Extranjero*, that we had just applied for were the most important documents we would need while owning a house in Spain.

The time was 1.45pm. We were due to be at Alicante airport for check-in by 4pm, and we still needed a mortgage to buy the house that we had already signed for.

Bill once again set off apace, his white trainers flashing in the sunlight. Bob helped me along as my heeled M&S sandals made running anywhere out of the question.

"Get in love," urged Bill "the bank closes at 2pm."

"But Bill," I pleaded, "Its 1.45 and we have those mountains to drive through. We'll never do it!"

Bill ignored me as he drove out of town and punched numbers into his phone to make a hands-free call.

We heard as the numbers formed a ringing sound and a man answered.

"Hi Bill, what can I do you for?" Bill smiled while selecting a cigarette with his teeth from its box and lit it. I hated it when he took even one hand off the wheel, and the mountain ravines didn't look inviting.

"Joseph, I need a favour. I need you to get to the bank manager and keep him talking until we get there, and can you do it quick-sharp?" There was a muffled sound which must have been

Joseph picking up his keys. "OK, over and out, on my way. That manager is SOOO cute!"

We were on our way to buy a Spanish mortgage.

As Bill knocked on the glass door of the bank, I could see a man standing by the cash machine.

Bob and I looked askance and just stood there as we blinked rapidly. It was more like a scene from Alice in Wonderland than a serious proposition for buying a house in another country. The man laughed at us and waved his hand.

Joseph greeted Bill warmly. This immaculately dressed, rather effeminate man sporting his Ray Bans on his receding hairline then launched into a whistle-stop tour of his renal problems, as he reiterated the conversation he had had with his consultant that morning. He giggled like a schoolgirl when I told him I really thought he was the bank manager.

Joseph put his manicured fingers to his lips and whispered to me conspiratorially, "Not me darling, but that gorgeous man in there is."

Unfortunately, the object of their desire had decided to keep one of his staff behind to interview us instead, and whether the manager had fled through the back door to escape Joseph we will never know.

Philippe introduced himself to us in perfect English and while Joseph and Bill went to the nearby restaurant to carry on the story of Joseph's entrails, we talked to Philippe.

Ten minutes later we were back out in the sunshine, clutching an elaborate file and a list of papers we needed to produce and send to Spain and, if we were not very much mistaken, a mortgage offer. We found Joseph and Bill and neither of our lunch companions were slightly surprised that we had a mortgage offer. Bill thrust a menu in front of us; this was to be our first meal on a very strange day. As Bob went to take the menu from Bill, Joseph grabbed it and declared, "None of that nonsense. I will order for you!" and with a wave and a whistle he called to the waiter.

"Manuel!"

Following a whirlwind lunch, with probably the best egg

and chips we'd ever had, Bill herded us into the car and once more, the car sped back up into the mountains. By the time we got back to Pego I felt very sick, likely due in equal measure to the stress of the day and the egg and chips. Bill, as ever, had the remedy and this time two mint teas solved the problem and my lunch settled as we waited to see a solicitor.

The solicitor's office was next to Bill's office. This relationship proved to be the weakest link in our chain. We entered her office with the perfunctory salutations. Esther's English was one hundred percent better than our Spanish, but only forty percent good enough for us to understand. She nodded a lot and said, "you see!" many times. The problem was, we didn't 'see' at all. She then took her stamp (every official person had one) and made black rings with tiny writing on many pieces of paper and then stood up and shook our hands with a "*Si, adios!*" – and that was it!

Bill unceremoniously bundled us out of the door, ushered us into his car, and perhaps thankfully we were too stunned to realise that much longer and we would have missed our flight.

All too soon we were back at Alicante airport, the folder we clung to for dear life full-to-bursting with documents from everyone we'd met, a list of questions we had to answer, an enormous to-do list and three miniature bottles of cava from Sandra at the estate agents. With tears in our eyes, we hugged Bill and proceeded to totter through passport control. We texted the kids, boarded the plane and I, usually an ace air traveller, for the first time in my life, vomited all the way home.

Chapter 4:

Casa de Sueños

As new parents are after a birth, we were very pleased with ourselves and could talk of very little else to friends and family. We were very nonchalant about the whole business - "Yes, that's right, we went to Spain for the weekend and bought a house – well, you know, a *casa* – that's Spanish for a house." We had decided to name our new Spanish home *Casa de Sueños* – House of Dreams.

We were like swans in those heady early days – on the surface, totally serene, while below the water we were paddling like mad. Documents flew across the continent at great speed – or rather, not at any great speed at all. Most of our papers were lost en route and tracking them was a nightmare. How many times did Bob hear from a very courteous mystery voice, "Yes, Mr Carter, your envelope was last tracked at Madrid Airport... No sir, we do not know what happened from there. Have a nice day." This was 2004, and even though within the UK, business transactions were being managed by electronic methods, our Spanish business dealings were still mostly carried out over fax or by snail mail.

Bob had to do most of the document filing and negotiations with Spain because even though the house would be in joint names, this being Spain, the man, *el hombre*, was paramount.

At least Philippe the bank clerk was emailing me, a good sign in many ways as we realised Spanish officials seemed to think that email is the work of the devil and faxes should be sent whenever possible. His emails were cheery, "Hello! It is nice weather again today. You will lose your mortgage now in three days if your documents do not arrive. Have a nice day."

Another set of payslips and documents were despatched and just when we thought the deadline had passed, still having received no word from Spain, poor Bob's cup was not only half empty, it was smashed to pieces. In his mind we had lost the house. I was philosophical and had been told by a fortune teller some years ago that she could see me acquiring a white house. I truly believed the house would be ours.

After enduring the longest 24 hours following the deadline, still we had heard nothing. I closed my eyes tight as I pressed 'send' on an email to Philippe, asking for an update. His reply…

"Oh yes, all the papers came together, they had been stuck in Madrid, they came two days ago. All is well, goodbye." Another lesson we learned the hard way – no-one tells you anything.

But hurray! The mortgage was in place and now we could move to completion.

We rang our Spanish lawyer but each time the call went to voicemail. It was years until we learned that calling between 8am-10am GMT was the best time if you had any hope of speaking to an official, as after that, siesta would intervene.

I emailed, adding 'high priority' red flags and 'URGENT' to each email. I faxed. I sent meditational thoughts to the cosmos. Eventually an email arrived – the English was questionable, but the message was clear.

"To complete this house, it must be three days' time you must be here both if not good then both give me Power of Attorney by two days or you have no house and you lose 3,000 euros."

Go directly to jail. Do no pass GO. Do not collect £200.

Flying back to Spain at such short notice was out of the question. I remembered speaking to my hairdresser – yes, hairdresser – who had told me that he had bought an apartment In Torrevieja a couple of years earlier and I remembered that he had mentioned enlisting a Power of Attorney lawyer. Thankfully, remembering that chat over a back-wash meant we were able to find a lawyer to act as a notary – who would, at short notice, receive the documents, have them translated and sent on to us ready for our signatures, then we would post them to Commonwealth House in London, then they would be sent by special delivery to the solicitor's little office in the hills of Pego! Again, we were told we could track our documents... Groundhog Day... "Yes, Mr Carter your envelope was last tracked at Madrid Airport. No sir, we do not know what happened from there. Have a nice day."

We waited 24 hours and then faxed our solicitor in Spain. I received a reply, "Yes, your documents, it is here."

Halleluiah!

On Monday 28 May 2004, 34 days after we had stood on the roof terrace, we were the proud owners of our very own *casa*! Hurrah! Despite the stress of telephone calls, faxes, emails (mainly no emails, as a matter of fact) sleepless nights, there we were – a two-property family.

We couldn't wait to go back – to touch our walls, to drink chilled wine on our roof terrace while watching the sun's daily visit to our little house, seeing where he chose to rest throughout the day, and where he liked to leave his mate, the shadow.

In June 2004 we were off. One of the consequences of having a second home was that I finally had to master the internet at home – at the office, much of it was done for me by my staff but since some of the service providers in Spain dealt in with correspondence in email (unless they chose not to, just like the solicitors and estate agents we were now used to dealing with), then I had to bite the bullet. This was much to the chagrin of our daughter Hayley who became my tutor, my guide, my fixer of my mistakes – all while in the middle of sitting her A Level exams.

Bill kindly suggested (in an email...!) that since we only had a weekend on our next visit that we should not hire a car and instead he would pick us up at Alicante Airport and take us home – home to our *casa*!

We checked the weather (on the internet! Hayley showed me how!) and a balmy 28°C was forecast. We knew we would have no air-conditioning, but we knew we had a nice fridge, so the wine would at least be cool. Armed with an electric fan and a can of Magicool spray in our luggage, we were fearless.

We touched down on Spanish soil, Bob dragging behind him the suitcase containing said fan, bedding and all sorts of paraphernalia that I had decreed might be of use. It was midnight when we hugged Bill and warm words and greetings spilled out from the three of us as Bill drove us back to our little bit of Polop de la Marina.

As we paid the motorway toll at junction 65A, Bill became exceptionally quiet. Then he coughed in a very theatrical manner, Bob and I waiting expectantly.

"What is it?!" Bob and I echoed. We felt Bill had something to tell us, but he just could not bring himself to do it.

All of a sudden, both of us were transported in our minds back to that awkward journey of the month before when Bill was driving us along this very route, up the coast from Murcia after that day of disappointing viewings. What a difference a day can make, let alone a month.

Distracted, and a little embarrassed, by the memory of that journey, we barely noticed where we were until the car came to a stop alongside out villa. Next thing we knew, Bill was popping across to his house to find a bottle of wine while Bob retrieved the cases from the car.

Here we are, then. Bob and I, all teary eyed, stood looking at our new front door with a mixture of anticipation, excitement and awe.

Bill hugged us and left us to enjoy our special moment.

Bob, ever the romantic, unlocked the door, picked me up and carried me over the threshold. As I held on to Bob, he tried to locate the light switch on the wall in the pitch-black. There was a click as he found it and switched it on, followed by almighty BANG.

Bob and I are often told that we are so right for each other that we emanate our own electricity – well, this wasn't that!

It was the fact that the lovely vendors had taken not only

the fridge, but the light fittings as well, and, in their hurry, had left wires touching. Luckily, I had a torch in the suitcase – of course I would!

Not to worry. Soon we had unpacked two glasses and retired to our sunroof with our now not-so-chilled bottle of wine! We celebrated the fact that Bob was lucky to be alive after his first brush with Spanish electrics. The kind Brits who had sold us our house had pushed for an early sale, cost us hundreds of pounds in fees in doing so, then nicked our fridge, robbed us of light and nearly killed my husband...

Welcome to Spain.

Litigation and Spain go together like traffic and the M25. Both sets are to be avoided at all costs. If there is one piece of advice that I would pass on to anyone purchasing a home in Spain, it would be to get yourself a good *gestor*. It's hard to explain what a *gestor* is, as we don't have an equivalent in the UK, but they are absolutely vital when it comes to navigating Spanish bureaucracy.

My second piece of advice would be to enlist a *gestor* who is prepared to:

-       Answer your calls
-       Answer your emails
-       Answer your English solicitors' calls and emails
-       Answer your Spanish bank's calls and emails
-       Tell you what they are doing on your behalf
-       Explain an action to you before they act upon it
-       Tell you when their offices open and close
-       Tell you that the documents that you have sent from England, costing the same amount of sterling as a trip around the world, have indeed, arrived safely.

In our ignorance, we foolishly allowed ourselves to be 'given' a *gestor* (it's a long story). I will call her Lester, although I have called her many other things in the past. By year two we had a brilliant *gestor*, called Hector, and Hector the *gestor* was to be our saviour on many occasions – but Lester, meanwhile...

We did insist that since we had not had the opportunity to

learn Spanish at that time, we needed an English-speaking *gestor*. We were assured, as we had been on many other matters, that not only did Lester speak fluent English, but she was competent at her job!

The following was a typical telephone conversation with Lester – but only if she happened to pick the phone up by mistake:

ME: Buenos Dias Lester (Silence.) Lester, are you there? Can you hear me?

LESTOR: (After some time.) ... Sí.

ME: That's good. Lester, please may I ask you a question?

LESTOR: Si, adios, goodbye.

I have since learned that Lester was not on her own in the art of making life as difficult as possible for us. The Spanish, when it comes to business... well! In my opinion, and according to our experiences at that time in 2004:

•   They don't 'do' email. Fax still rules OK - but they don't read them.

•   They don't like to meet with you so it's no use saying, "I will jump on a plane and come to see you *right now!*" They won't be available when you get there. Even if you previously arranged, and agreed, an appointment.

•   There's a never a good time to get hold of them. First thing in the morning they do their admin so are un-available to speak to you by phone, so you leave a message. They pick that up about 11am but they must wait at least two hours before they call you back, by which time it is Siesta time. They come back to the office around 5pm our time, at which point we have left the office. Oh, whoops, there's another day gone. Siestas for workers in the field I can understand – but bank clerks? Council office workers? Solicitors? *Gestors*? No!

Tradesmen, now they are a different kettle of *pescados*. Get a good one and the work, (unless its building a house) will be exceptionally well done, as it is a matter of honour.

Chapter 5:

Living the dream

Buying a holiday home is fraught; it will age you, it will stress you out, it will give you tension in places you didn't think possible.... but then, sitting on your sun terrace at dusk, sipping from a chilled bottle of white Rioja, it all feels worthwhile...

Until you meet the neighbours.

Spanish neighbours are uncomplicated. They'll put up fences around their property, they will nod '... dias' and 'hola.' They will have yapping dogs that they will leave out in the midday sun, in the rain and in the snow (because it does rain and snow, but no-one tells you). They will not clean up their dog's poo, (no wonder they don't have carpets), but their children will not cause you a nuisance. They will sound like they are having a domestic row at any time of day when in fact they are asking each other if they would like a cup of coffee. They will have visitors who will block your driveway with their car, even if you are stood by your car, keys in hand, waiting to drive off. If you have a structural problem with your house or roof tiles damaged or a leak, they will all come and have a look, scratch their heads and rub their chins, shake their heads and convey to you that this is the worst thing in the world – then they'll shake your hand and go back home.

Fiestas mean fireworks, where you can watch from your roof terrace as they light a blue touch paper of a firework with a match in one hand and a cigarette in the other. Apart from the cruelty to their animals, I like the Spanish as neighbours.

Brit neighbours fall into two categories. The first, the holiday lets and the holiday home owners, happy to be there, taking over the communal pool, throwing cans off the sun terrace, asking you where the nearest sports bar is - sometimes vomiting outside your door overnight. At least that set are transient and disappear for days on end when the third-degree sunburn takes hold.

The second should have a government health warning... expats. They know everything, they don't try to speak the language, they hunt for new Brit neighbours in packs. First the scout is sent out, they'll pass your house on a leisurely stroll to the bin, (they must search high and low for litter to take to the bin) then, they make eye contact... boom! Gotcha!

"Hello... you moved in then? We wondered who would buy it at such a high price, ours was a bargain."

If you are foolish enough to reply, the scout will lean on the gate, hoping... bingo! It's not locked, and they accidently fall in. First move completed, he has safely crossed the first check point. Moving forward as quickly as possible to shake your hand, with a hop, skip and a jump – yes, he's on your front terrace. Now, to ingratiate himself to you...

Before you have time to speak, he will be utterly amazed to see his wife, Janice, at your gate.

You are now caught in the hunter's trap. There is no route of escape.

Janice, no doubt will be wearing something flowing in iridescent pink or orange, clanking bracelets, skin looking like leather, no sunglasses but with such dried skin that her eyes must be searched for on her face.

Janice is even more surprised to see her husband, who she's been 'searching for all over', even though he has only been gone from their house for three minutes.

While you are secretly trying to come up with a reason why you suddenly need to go out (but damn, the Spanish neighbours have blocked the driveway), they will move in for the interrogation phase. Painlessly and for reasons beyond your control, you are compelled to tell them why you have bought that house in particular, how much it cost. They in turn will advise you on who you should know, who you should keep away from – especially the Spanish.

While the Spanish keep their dogs outside, the Brit expat keeps his satellite dish outside. Size is everything, the bigger the better. In fact, on urbanisations the carport is actually a satellite dish docking station.

The conversation, or should I say, speech, on your terrace will carry on something like ours did that fateful day.

"We bought before the boom, best thing ever. You never have to eat anything Spanish, there's loads of Brit supermarkets – dearer, mind, but well, who cares? Who wants that foreign muck when you can get faggots from Iceland."

"Or I get my mam to bring a couple of frozen lamb leg joints when she is coming over from Leeds. Nice and defrosted by the time she's arrived."

The day of this first encounter, we were exhausted, and extremely hot. We were standing in the blistering heat while they enjoyed the coolness of our new front patio awning, and even though we really didn't want to hear any more 'help', there was an expectant silence as they stood looking at us.

"Would you... like a drink?"

The reply at first gave us some hope, but then, we were doomed.

"Well no, don't worry, we don't want to keep you... oh but go on then, if you insist, thanks mate. Best let the girls talk Bob, I am sure your missus will want to know about the Chinese shop and the lovely stuff you can get there. They've got those vases with bright painting all over them, one of them would look a treat instead of that old brown jug you have there, you see them everywhere here, the Spanish use them a lot, God knows what for, never seen the attraction myself. Now Bob... any risqué DVDs in your collection there, nudge nudge, wink wink... cold winter nights... you know?"

Argh! Trapped forever, while he sifted through my Catherine Cookson and audibly sighed at Bob's John Wayne collection.

Soon after, we had another very similar experience and so, with haste, we employed a Spanish company to fit a high wrought-iron gate to the front and side of our property. We didn't know the Spanish for machine gun turrets or we would have had those affixed too.

The work was done on time and looked fabulous. We paid in cash and shortly after he'd merrily driven away, we realised he had forgotten just one tiny thing – to fit a lock. Without it, we'd be back where we started – there'd just be a higher gate for the neighbour to push.

We rang the workman so he could come and rectify it but, of course, he never replied. Undaunted, we bought a padlock from the Chinese shop for one euro. We went for one without bright painting all over it.

Chapter 6:
Furniture

Given that the only piece of furniture our lovely Brit predecessors had left us was a very rickety double bed, on our third weekend out to *Sueños*, our mission was to buy furniture. I had always remonstrated when we had been to the East (of the world, that is) that people coming to and from the UK had the largest suitcases I had ever seen, and probably had their Grandma stowed away in theirs. Later on, you will read another tale concerning suitcases and flesh but, for now, the concern was furnishing our new purchase. So, in preparation, I bought two enormous suitcases.

I was never a girl scout but perhaps, in another life, I was a Sherpa, as I suddenly discovered a talent for hauling all kinds of things over to Spain for the villa. This was 2004, before airlines started charging you for breathing mid-flight; I had 10kg available in each hand luggage bag and 22kg in each suitcase. This amazing 64kg of carriage weight was FREE!

Therefore, in the hand luggage I had the following:
- Bed Linen
- Curtains
- Towels
- Soap
- Hangers
- Candles (in case more lights had been stolen)
- Various picture frames
- Sponges
- Cleaning materials
- Pillows.

Bob was permitted a little of his clothing in his hand luggage, along with a few of my knickers and my spare make-up.

In the suitcases, I packed:

- Telescope curtain rails
- Bob's tool box
- Hammer
- Brush with long handle
- Bedside cabinets (dismantled and flat-packed by Bob)
- A computer desk (as above)
- An occasional table (as above)
- A steam blower for the garden
- Another fan
- Two collapsible clothes rails.

On my person, I wore:

- A swimsuit
- Two vests
- Two t-shirts
- A jumper
- A pair of jeans
- A pair of jogging bottoms
- A cardigan around my waist
- A jacket
- Two pairs of socks
- I additionally carried a coat, an umbrella and a cushion (which I told the cabin crew that I needed to lean on in-flight)

Bob would not adhere to joining me in this endeavour, his lame excuse being that he had to carry a mere 64kg of furniture/household wares...

We were very excited as, on the evening of our arrival, Bill and Pete were having a small dinner party, outside (oh! Outside! So Spanish!). Bill had also been out and bought us a fabulous fridge and had installed some light fittings for us. God Bless Bill, it was hardly his fault that we had been 'done' and, literally, left in the dark, but he took it upon himself and felt responsible. We were, and always will be, grateful to him.

We unpacked, and Bob stood incredulous as the 'Mary Poppins' case brought forth furniture, an array of electricals and fancy goods – as well as a Warburton's loaf, some margarine and a pack of bacon!

We changed (well, I took off a few layers) and off we strolled to our neighbours'. The crickets chirped, the cicadas sang, the stars twinkled; so many stars. The evergreens on the mountain filled our lungs – well, at least mine, as Bob's and Bill's needed room for the Silk Cut.

Candles added a fairy glow and the aromas from the barbecue made our mouths water in anticipation. Conversation was easy, and we were given a sermon on which neighbours to avoid (although we had already had that initiation ourselves), who to be nice to but "remember to keep walking as you talk."

I was also beginning to learn quite quickly that some expats in Spain led very odd lives sometimes, and perhaps fled the UK in order to hide – usually an addiction or a predilection. As always, I wanted to be part of the conversation, and so I mentioned how lovely one our neighbours, Samantha, was and how sorry I was to hear about her terrible fall and the subsequent stitches she had in her forehead. "It must be really awful for her, I bet she has to explain that she fell and that she hadn't been lamped (a northern phrase for 'struck') by her wife-beating husband! Ha!" The silence fell heavier than the dew on the mountains behind us.

I knew to move on very quickly, so gushed on about our excitement at going shopping in the morning for our furniture. This was the last time we would be over in Spain without a hire car and we honestly expected that we would simply call a taxi to take us down to the retail park where the large shops lived, about four kilometres away. Bill explained that taxis didn't yet venture to the Urbanisation as it was so new and unknown, and preferred easy fares from holidaymakers by the coast. Bill had been called to the office the next morning and Pete, still in his right-hand drive car, had already committed to drive a neighbour elsewhere.

"No matter," Pete volunteered, "Julie here will give you a lift tomorrow, won't you, Julie?" Poor Julie, still evidently unsure how to handle me and listing slightly to one side, looked (wine) glassy-eyed into the distance.

"Yes, just come around about 9am. I'll take you."

With our transport arrangements sorted, we bid our fellow diners and hosts goodnight and, hand-in-hand, took the short stroll back across the road to our abode.

It was stiflingly hot, and the old bed was uncomfortable; but we were soon lulled to sleep by the sound of our whirring fans. We slept through until we were awoken with a start by the next-door neighbour's dog's daily barking alarm call.

At 9am the next morning, all was still very quiet over at Julie's house. Bob and I decided it was prudent not to knock at our new neighbour's door given the likelihood of a hangover, so we set to work on clearing the weeds in the front garden with the hope she would eventually see us and know we were ready. By 10am, there was still no sign. As siesta starts anytime from 1pm onwards, furniture buying time was short. The following day was Saturday, where the shops shut completely at 1pm, then Sunday, when nowhere would be open, and we flew back on Monday.

Getting slightly anxious, eventually I decided to give her gate a courteous rumble but nothing stirred. As with all villas in Spain, there was a black wrought iron door, then a wooden door - the exception being our frontage, where our predecessors were either the only residents not to have one, or, like the fridge, cooker and light fittings, they had taken it with them.

I slid my fingers through the wrought iron and knocked on the wooden door. As I did so, it swung slowly open and in the dimness of the shuttered house I could see what looked like a large fleece throw, half on the sofa and half on the floor. Suddenly the fleece slid to the floor and, like Gollum from Lord of the Rings, slithered its way across the floor towards me. Heart pounding, I realised that the vision was my new neighbour, Julie. She reached the door, still prostrate on the marble floor tiles, and through the wrought-iron exterior door came her clammy hand, a business card between her fingers. I took it from her, and with a loud burp she turned and made her way back along the floor to the sofa.

I ran back across the road to Bob and showed him the card, which, as it transpired, was for a taxi firm. We dialled the number and, after a while, finally made ourselves understood.

We arrived at the furniture store, relieved to see the prices of the furniture were cheaper than the taxi fare we had just paid.

Buying the furniture was surreal; hues and designs we would never have dared live with in the UK seemed right and proper in this colourful country. A large, red, L-shaped suite was the first piece that caught our eye. Bob and I spotted, eagle-like, that another pasty-skinned couple, obviously expat virgins, had spotted it too and were about to beat a pathway to it. Stealthily, I made my way through the store, negotiating tables and chairs and bookcases faster than the speed of light (well, almost) and threw myself unceremoniously across one side of the sofa. I glared menacingly at the couple, who stopped in their tracks and obviously decided that if the mad woman wanted it, they didn't.

A bed, table and chairs followed. NatWest security must have noticed our many purchases and telephoned me to see if my card had been stolen. I assured them that it hadn't, but "my husband might soon be hoping it was". After a reviving *menú del día* lunch, comprising six courses and half a bottle of wine each for just 9 euros, we were ready to take on Carrefour supermarket!

The supermarket, or *hipermercado*, has a special place in expats' eyes; it is the Mecca for all things household and grocery. When you became a seasoned expat, you hardly ever go in, even if you want to, and certainly not if you have friends over from the UK. You would want them to see you ordering your bread from the *panadería* and your chickens, *asado*, from the butcher – and doing a lot of meaningful sniffing of fruit and veg, chatting to the street vendors. We loved the old gentleman in Benidorm who sold his fruit from a cart; like us in the early days, holidaymakers would believe he was the epitome of 'real Spain' and would buy their kilo of fruit (whether true or not, he claimed not to speak English – so you could never buy just one piece). It was only as the sun got high in the sky and they turned to their citrus swag bag that they would find the contents mouldy, or worse, coming alive, crawling around the other picnic items. Of course, by that time the man and his barrow would be long gone for his Siesta and no doubt off to the local supermarket for the bargain out-of-date fruit for his *mañana* barrow.

We still love Carrefour hypermarket. Afterall, you don't need to know the Spanish for sieve or ironing board; you just put them in your trolley. The supermarket resembles an aircraft hangar with the brightest lights possible so that you miss nothing. The shop floor assistants are on roller skates which means if you ask them a question in English, they can get away from you as quickly as possible while shrugging their shoulders at the same time, bless 'em!

Back to our *muebles casa* day. We were in Carrefour for five hours; with two trolleys full, we finally left the Aladdin's cave to find a taxi. Bob comforted me when I realised that the shopping centre did indeed sell everything, including puppies and kittens and birds, all clinically cooped up in the smallest of glass boxes.

The spring sunshine had been seduced to its own siesta and the sky was as grey as our ironing board cover. Large droplets of rain transformed it into a polka dot pattern.

The taxi queue was enormous and, we noticed, as we stood outside getting wetter and wetter, no taxis were coming anyway. Our first experience of "the rain in Spain falls mainly... everywhere!"

I used to be an assistant TV drama editor and I always used to complain that the 'rain' they used in rainy-day scenes, gushing down as if from fire engine water-hoses, never looked like real. Well, obviously all the directors were Spanish!

We had managed to cover the trolleys with plastic bags and we soon looked like we had been swimming in the sea. My dress, made of viscose, which previously had, in my opinion, demurely skimmed my calves, was shrinking fast and would soon be nothing more than a blouse. In desperation, we rang Bill. "No worries," he said, "I'm on my way." We waited sheepishly like two naughty children for 'Uncle Bill' to once again be our knight in shining armour. When we spied him, we waved madly to him as he turned into the car park before any other of his friends jumped in (Bill seemed to know everyone), and we apologised over and over, soon covering the inside of his car windows in a warm, damp mist.

It was time to go home; all the furniture had been ordered and would be delivered in five weeks. Big hugs, lots of slapping of backs and we left with a promise that we would hire a car next time. We were off back to Blighty.

Before our *casa* sales trip to Spain, the one where we were not going to get sold to, we had booked to spend a week in a caravan (sorry! A mobile home!) in the South of France, along with Bob's elder brother, David and our daughter, Hayley, during her last summer holiday before heading off to university. The same South of France, where only three months before we had told everyone we were going to buy our holiday home and to where poor David and Hayley were told to purchase their plane tickets. Now all had changed, and we had a house in Spain!

The rest of our children, still recovering from the shock, had their own holidays planned, so I changed David's and Hayley's air tickets, told them not to bring too many clothes and happily snaffled their baggage allowance for more furniture to be brought out, including a chest of drawers (yes – the shell in one case, draws in the other), a collapsible standard lamp, table lights, wastepaper bins, garden furniture... need I go on?

Hayley's forte at school was languages and so we thought her knowledge of Spanish would come in handy for all the questions we still had and David, as well as being a pack horse for household goods, could also help Bob with the DIY.

We were now in July of 2004 and the heat was scorching as we emerged from Alicante Airport. We had hired a people-carrier car, more for transporting our baggage than for people, but the air conditioning was welcomed by all. We knew we had one night at *Sueños* without air conditioning, as the units were due to be fitted the following day. So that night, while Dave and Bob had the use of the only working fan in the spare bedroom, Hayley and I had only a tin of 'Magicool' to spray on ourselves every hour to prevent spontaneous combustion.

Next morning, the two young men arrived to fit our dual-purpose air conditioning and heating units. Bob and I didn't believe we required the heating part, but Bill had insisted, so we bowed to his superior knowledge. How grateful we would be when the thermometer dropped during the winter months and we would be cosy in our *casa* – the marble floors so welcome in summer were deathly to the feet in winter.

Bob and I had a master plan; no doubt the two Spanish young men would be prepared to do a little cash-in-hand work, so we decided to ask them if they would fit the lovely outside carriage lights we had bought in our haul from Carrefour. Well actually, we weren't going to ask them – we thought Hayley could, and just to ensure that they were hooked to do this, we suggested she wear her cutest bikini and sunbathed outside the house. David would hang around as chaperone, and we would leave Hayley with some euros to pay the young men.

Darling Hayley was still learning Spanish and had not acquired a full vocabulary at that point, so she had to phrase her questions using the words she knew. She had therefore said to the young men in her best Spanish, "When you have finished this work, I have something I would like you both to do for me."

As one might guess, the boys had the units working in all the rooms in no time at all.

Hayley, to her horror, thinking of the error she might have implied and realising her uncle was snoring away in one of the bedrooms, then decided it would be imprudent to go into the house while the young men were finishing off their work, so she therefore stayed outside in the midday sun.

On our return, we noticed two very disappointed looking

young Spaniards driving away in their van, all the outside lights fitted, and Hayley, sitting under the cool of the air conditioning unit in our lounge, with calamine poultices on her sunburned skin.

The following day, the furniture was due to arrive at 5pm, so we decided we would have a holiday-day rather than just doing DIY – that way, perhaps Hayley might just forgive us. We had a lovely morning on the beach (with Hayley's sunburn responsibly covered) and then took them for lunch for lunch, and we all happily chomped through another six courses with wine.

We drove home, tired but content, and waited for the furniture to arrive. Right on time the van arrived, and two men shoved an invoice under my nose. I duly took the thin pink piece of paper and nodded knowledgably as if I could read the Spanish carbon copy. I saw my signature at the bottom, which was good enough for me, and waved them in.

Our excitement didn't last long. It turned out that the beautiful red suite, the fantastic black wrought-iron dining table with glass top etc etc... were all in flat packs!

Once again Bob and I stood in our Spanish lounge, scratching our heads and wondering what the hell to do.

David and Hayley, recognising the storm brewing across Bob's forehead, disappeared to their respective bedrooms, switched on their respective aircon units, and had a nap. Bob walked outside to have a calming cig and to think.

A couple of cigs later, the clouds clearing, he came back into the lounge with his B&Q battery-charged screwdriver (brought out by me in the luggage) and set to work. With me as his labourer, it took us two hours while we unpacked the boxes, which filled our entire lounge, worked out which way up the instruction booklet pictures were meant to face, counted out screws and washers from the little plastic packets and, now and again, I would have to utter, "sorry love I can't hold this side much longer...", or "do you need another plaster?" But, we did it!

Hayley appeared first and, so excited to see our work – she

said it looked like the elves had been to work while she slept. Then David came in, rubbing his eyes.

"You've done well there. What's for tea?"

Slowly but surely, in fact, in record time, our *casa* took on the personality of a home.

Bob's job, and mine, were, and still are, intrinsically linked, and at that time we both worked in the media and charity sectors. We had a portfolio of roles, which had led us to meet in the first place. It meant that our individual contact books were an enviable mixture of business people, heads of charities, council officials, nobility and celebrities. While we never took our celebrity friends for granted, it still came as a surprise to us when our other friends excitedly pointed out magazine pages of us photographed in their company at society events. I had remembered that on one such occasion an actor friend of ours mentioned that he had been invited and attended a personal appearance (or a 'PA', as it is known in the trade) at a venue just outside of Benidorm and had a fabulous time.

I telephoned the owner of the establishment which was, and still is, known as 'Benidorm Palace'. I explained who we were, and she very kindly invited us to go along and visit the venue when we were next over. As a sojourn from DIY, Bob, David, Hayley and I went along one evening. As is usual for such an occasion, we had dressed in smart clothes and, as can happen in Benidorm, people in smart clothes can stand out slightly – but not at this venue. It was nothing like a bingo emporium, as we had wryly anticipated. We didn't have wifi at that time, so we had no way of 'checking it out' in advance. It is still fondly known as the Las Vegas of Spain, and I think that is an apt title.

Our expectation, or lack thereof, of some of our lovely fellow Brit holidaymakers and their wardrobe choices might seem mean. Believe me, now, after over a decade, I can speak with some insider knowledge. Some still wear their summer holiday attire even if the weather is inappropriate, so an evening in 'Brit Land' Benidorm means, in the main, short denim skirts for women under 30 – if the legs are going a bit then its three quarter length shorts – teamed with a brightly-coloured boob tube (oh yes, they are still popular out there...so to speak), flip flops and big hoop earrings which double for hula-hoops and come in very handy for hoop-la, if the funfair is in town. The male of the species wears someone else's name, usually a footballer's, on their shirt, which has cost the earth. The Spanish over-40s on the other hand, who, yes, do go to SOME streets in 'Brit Land', will, by seven o'clock, have a sludge-coloured coat on to ward off the sea breeze when it's still 20°C. Bob and I have mused that there is a missing generation within the Spanish community. When the *señoritas*, with their olive skin and seductive toss of their jet-black curly locks, reach 29 years old, they are lead into a big factory and come out the other end at 30 weighing five stones heavier, their hair chopped off and dyed muddy orange to match their beige-coloured coat or anorak, under which is their beachwear – a black swimsuit with big flowers on. When sunbathing, many are known to stand with legs apart and wee straight into the Mediterranean. The Scandinavians dress well, mainly in sports gear, but after all during the day they are partaking in some sort of outdoor pursuit and in the evening, they go to nice restaurants!

The Spain of the 1950s was a very different place to the 'wear what you like', anything goes, society that we have today. In the rock and roll years, the feared Guardia Civil and the Catholic Church ensured that a strict moral code was observed, and simply wearing a bikini on the beach, even by a tourist, could lead to a large fine, or even worse!

The story of how the then-Mayor of Benidorm, Pedro Zaragoza, got on his scooter and rode to Madrid to ask General Franco for permission to exempt his beloved Benidorm from these rules is recorded in history books. Surprisingly, Franco agreed. This fascinating story of a young mayor's fight to make a resort that was attractive to more European visitors was made into a short film by Nakamura Films. Mayor Zaragoza is played by actor Sergio Caballero and is entitled 'Bikini'. No doubt you can find it on

YouTube.

This same visionary mayor created the *Plan General de Ordenación Urbana Benidorm* in 1954, guaranteeing every building an area of leisure land. From the Sierra Helada, the promontory at the end of the Rincon de Loix, you can really see how green the city is. Considering Spain was not long out of the civil war, the growth of the city was surprisingly well planned. The city was planned to grow vertically so that, as well as ensuring space between buildings to let light in, it was also done to reward as many visitors as possible with a view of the sea. The roads were planned with much forethought for expansion. At one time, there was a plan to give the Avenida de Mediterráneo eight lanes of traffic! Due to a public outcry, the road plans were reduced to six lanes. How far-sighted were the planners, when at that time there were only seven car owners registered in the entire city. The Avenida crosses the resort from the Levante right through to the old town. Certainly, in the height of summer, Bob and I would like another couple of lanes on that road, especially at lunchtime when we want to have our picnic on the beach!

The house was coming on nicely, and I already had a list of what I needed to bring out next time. David and Bob put together two outside benches and painted them while Hayley weeded, and I busied myself sewing curtain hems and moving shelves to fit in our crockery, all brought from home of course.

On our last night, we decided to take our two team members for a meal to treat them for the work they had put in during the week. We went to the local Chinese restaurant that we had visited on our last time over; we were keen to show Team David and Hayley one of our culinary finds.

"Have anything you like on the menu," said my generous husband.

"Thanks Dad," smirked Hayley, "big deal... the menu is only three euros for all you can eat, including a half a bottle of wine."

Bob and me, of course, thinking we had been clever locals

who had visited here before, had not realised that back then we had chosen from the 'à la tourist' menu and not the 'à la locals' one, which was hidden at the back. Ah well, we realised we had much to learn – but wasn't it all good fun.

All too soon, it was time to drive to the airport for our journey back to our other life. As we drove into the car rental car park, a young Spaniard, taking the wrong turn down a one-way, ran smack into us. We were yards from returning the car, and the perpetrator had sped off.

We were much shaken. Fortunately, the car hire representative had seen it happen. With a shrug of the shoulders, he took our paperwork and waved us on our way with a "Is OK, it is hired to someone else *mañana*, who cares, bye bye."

Chapter 7:

Village Life

And so, our parallel life began. At home in the UK, we thought fondly of our home in the sun, and vice versa. There were still so many operational challenges to overcome and we thought the time would never come when we could simply skip on a plane with a small bag each, hop off at Alicante airport and jump into our own car, driving off into the sunset.

We enjoyed our first winter trip immensely and were delighted that, since the hire car company had few customers that time of year, we were offered a rather nifty, iridescent green metallic car with doors that slid sideways instead of outwards. I can't remember the make, but they never did catch on. We mused that we could have suggested to the motor company that they have could employed our following experience as it would have made a terrific advert and might just have saved the model from extinction.

The Sunday of that trip, we decided to explore our neighbouring town of La Nucia, where there was a fabulous weekly *rastro*, or market, that had been part of the community for many years. We had been in the summer and immersed ourselves in a bit of real Spain. Every year for decades, and probably even longer, the farm workers have come down to nearer the coast to escape the searing summer heat of the interior, the markets around the towns providing them with an opportunity to sell anything and everything imaginable in a bid to feed their families.

That Sunday, there were stalls with heaps of clothes for one Euro, and so many lace table clothes and mantles obviously used in churches in years gone by. Religious artefacts abounded, as no doubt they will continue to for decades, and farm implements, too, which have lasted through many generations of killing, skinning and preparing farm animals for consumption. The stalls that, to this day, attract Bob and me, are the leather, denim and fur stalls. Where do they get all the fur coats from? In Spain? Where? Yes, it can get cold in winter but even the animals who wore the skins in the first place would gladly dispose of them if they could as the thermometer rises. Likewise, the leather coats...who wore them and where did they live?

I can still recall that first January market day when Bob had considered having me surgically removed from one stall – well, to say 'stall' is perhaps a little generous as it was actually a space with a rug on the ground and a coat-stand displaying various items. There it was, a size 8, blue leather coat by Dior for just 3 euros....

"If only it were a size 12," I wailed. On many a sleepless night since, I have berated myself for not buying it any way. I do still sport my one Euro denim jacket, though, with immense pride!

We bought our *café con leche* and doughnut from the tiny café by the entrance to the market, and how local we felt. We returned to the café many times afterwards, until the area became gentrified some five years later and the market moved to a new home. On entering the market café, the market stall holders – obviously all males – would be sitting in a line, each one a replica of the other, each with a glass of very strong coffee, a brandy and a cigarillo. The café owner was brusque and would never serve us if there was a local anywhere in the queue, ignoring us until they were all served. Over the ensuing few years, we gamely entered into the challenge of getting him to even acknowledge us. By year four or five, we would get a slight movement of the head by way of recognition – but perhaps we imagined it! We would sit outside on the plastic seats, perched precariously because the ground was so uneven, but we were living, for that one moment in time, as locals.

My Bob soon became adept at driving everywhere, even negotiating compact, winding streets, so we thought we would have a look at La Nucia itself since we had become regulars at the market. We knew that if we found the church square, we would find the action... as it were.

The short but precarious drive down to the church square was a breeze. The sun was shining, the bells tolled, but as Bob skilfully turned the corner into the church square, we came bonnet to fetlock with the most beautiful Spanish horses and their riders, equally majestic in the white shirts, leather waistcoats and fedoras. Bob brought the car to an abrupt holt and the riders reciprocated by doing the same to their steeds. As the horsemen moved to the flanks of our car, we realised that behind them was a parade of goats, people with cats in baskets, dogs, birds in cages, parrots on shoulders, children carrying fish tanks...

Soon, we were surrounded. Bob looked like the proverbial rabbit in headlights (which curiously was not part of the parade) and I had covered my face with my hands, peeping through my fingers. Not that anyone was looking at us, as they had seemed to accept our bright green metallic car as part of the parade. As the crowds moved behind us Bob inched the car forward and from stage left came a marching brass band which led us through the square and up the steep narrow road back to the main road. The band turned and returned to the square – and we carried on driving down the main road!

We later found out that dogs, cats, rabbits and even iguanas, many decked out in colourful sweaters to keep warm, troop into Spanish churches on the second or third Sunday in January for a blessing on the Day of Saint Anthony of Abbot, patron Saint of animals. I thought it was St Francis that got that gig but apparently not in such parts of Spain! Apparently, each year, pet-owners line up around the block of the Church of San Anton in central Madrid, awaiting the priest who stands at the entrance to bless their animals.

This was the catalyst we needed to buy our first car abroad.

Our search for our motor in the sun had begun.

We had only a little money left and so wanted a 'little run around' which we would keep at the airport ready for our 'hopping off' the plane and 'jumping into' car phase to begin. Our neighbour, Pete, had brought his car over from UK and we marvelled in those early days as he negotiated the Benidorm maze and all the surrounding mountains and still remembered which side of the road he should be on when his steering wheel was on the right. For us, it could only be a left-hand drive.

Once again, the stark contrasts of Spain were reflected in car sales. We found the area where all the standard dealerships were and soon realised it was not for us, given that we didn't have 12,000 euros upwards to spend.

Our budget was about 3,000 euros. We looked at the used-car markets, 'markets' being the operative word - *rustica* land bought cheap, the shell of a *finca* at one side where the guard dog was tied up, trying to escape the merciless midday sun. The other side of the area filled with very dusty cars. Keeping any car clean in Spain is a fulltime job!

Sadly, the dust in these cases were keeping the cars together. As every used-car 'market' looked the same, we wondered if we were in fact in Groundhog Day, as, each time, we were welcomed by an elderly man looking exactly like the last one, pulling up his baggy grey trousers to under his armpits, waving and walking over to us saying -

"Which one you want? Good price, *sí*?"

"Yes! A good price." We would then ask the price, and he would reply in Spanish. I would thumb quickly through my *Rapid Spanish for Beginners* book, and nothing resembled any numbers I could find. We had learned the Spanish word for all-important air conditioning, *acondicionada*, as driving in Spain without air conditioning is not recommended.

"*Sí*, all have!" gesticulated our car salesman, encompassing all the cars on show.

"*Bueno*," I say, "This one?"

"Eh no, not that."

"Well, this one?"

"Eh, no."

"OK, which ones?"

"*Sí*, all, *todos!*"

"OK, thanks, *adiós*…"

We tried so valiantly to buy from Spanish people, but, in the end, we resorted to a garage owned by an English couple. We bought a car which, just like our last hire car, happened to be bright green. She was called 'Twingo' and was a lady of a certain age.

My brother, 'Young' Ernie (who, incidentally, stands at 6ft 2 while my dear departed Dad, 'Big Ernie', stood at 5ft 9) and his wife Sheila, had come to visit us and came with us on the day we collected the car. We had purchased our car insurance, plus car breakdown cover, at a higher cost than in the UK (who said it was cheaper abroad?!) and all the necessary forms had been completed for the ITV (the Spanish equivalent of MOT). Bob drove us up to the garage in the hire car and then I, yes, me, after just one lesson from Bob about driving in Europe, drove Twingo back to our house.

Not only did we have a second home, we now had a second car… get us!

We had negotiated with the dealers to put a CD player in the car, but we discovered it had been put in vertically, meaning that if we drove over a hump in the road, the inserted CD popped out. What fun!

The following day, we took great pride in the fact that we were able to take Ernie (I will drop the 'Young', as he was 65 at the time) and Sheila back to the airport in Twingo and, on the way back, with no humps on the motorway, we were able to tune into our learning Spanish CD that Ernie and Sheila had bought us for Christmas. At that time, we hadn't cottoned on to the mysteries and vagaries of the area and its *patois*. Where we lived was in the *Communidad Valenciana*, and many people spoke Valenciano while many others in Spain speak Castilian Spanish – what we

Brits know as Spanish. More on the consequences of this later, but now, back to our learning!

The part of the CD taught us how to say "sorry" – "*lo siento*" – and "where is the airport?" and "the car has broken down" – "*el coche está roto*". This came in very handy as, the day before we were due to depart, we packed up the car with our beach gear and, you've guessed it – "*el coche está roto*"! This phrase proved useful from the off, as not only did we need to say it to the breakdown assistance lady, but when the engineer came to see us, his huge lorry negotiating our narrow road, he told us that the battery was "*roto*" – which we understood perfectly. He happened to have one in the enormous lorry and, 400 euros later, we signed a pink form and Twingo was once again ready to take to the roads.

There were many reasons why we had decided to store the car at one of the parking sites next to Alicante Airport. The first being the fact that there was a young English family living next door to us – it was their permanent home, and their two boys obviously liked to play in our garden when we weren't there. The giveaway was when the youngest asked me, "What are you doing living in our playground?"

The second reason comes back to our 'hop off plane, jump in car, drive home' dream.

We had chosen a company we called Albertos. We drove the car to Albertos, signed some papers, handed over 360 euros, bid *adiós* to Twingo, and were taken by minivan to the airport terminal. We were very proud of ourselves.

Some weeks later, we landed at Alicante Airport with just our hand luggage (although I was, of course, wearing two coats, three jumpers and had a cushion strapped to my person), so we hopped off the plane and were picked up by a minivan, ready to jump into Twingo. Well, we jumped into Twingo, but sadly Twingo was stationary and *en route* to nowhere. We called out to the receptionist in the makeshift office and told her "*el coche está roto!*" She got in the car and turned the key and said something which meant "your battery is *roto!*"

Finally, someone came and jump-started the car and off we

tootled home – not quite the 'jump' we had expected. We spoke to the car dealer and they explained, "Ah well, if you leave a car here in the tremendous heat, the battery needs to be ticked over."

After a few months of jumping into the car with hand luggage, the car going nowhere and then having to tip a guy to jump-start it, we decided to sell it.

We asked the car dealer if they could sell Twingo for us but, sadly, after her being back on their books for a year, no-one wanted our green goddess. In the end, Bill and Pete once again came to our aid and found us a private sale. They did, however, decide to finally change Pete's UK car for a left-hand drive. They didn't fancy Twingo, but Pete found a car he was happy with and, being thrifty, decided aircon wasn't necessary. When the chill of winter comes to Costa Blanca it's hard to imagine those blistering days of high summer that begin around April and stay through to September. So we were amused to see Pete, next time we were in Spain, driving along with a desk fan attached to his dashboard!

Driving in Spain along the well-kept roads across the mountains is a joy, most of the time. It can be more nail-biting when it's nearly siesta time, as there is such urgency to get home to *mama* for lunch and a sleep!

Chapter 8:

New Friends

Meeting new people and making friends is not unusual in everyday life but doing so while having a foot in two countries is, once again, part of the dual existence that we quickly became used to. Old friends in the UK looked stonily ahead when we mentioned our latest escapade with our friends in Spain. We looked forward to the day when real Spanish friends outnumbered expat-friends, however, to our merit, the friends we had formed ties with had lived in Spain for over 30 years so were almost Spanish… in our minds anyway. They did not live in expat enclaves either! They had beautiful *rustica* properties set into hillsides, which would all be the perfect backdrop for celebrity interviews in magazines like OK! or Hello. These people had come to Spain in 70s for myriad reasons, each worth a chapter of their own.

We start with 'Captain Jack', as we nicknamed him, head of a local English-language newspaper and a truly flamboyant character (hence his nickname, after Captain Jack Sparrow). I liked the paper and contacted him to sell the idea of me writing a regular column. For me, the paper was a cut above the rest, although, as time went on, I learned that all the English-language periodicals had their place.

Jack replied to me very quickly and on our next sojourn to Spain, I visited him at his offices. At reception, I was met by a formidable lady called Lyn, who was obviously the matriarch of the whole operation. I found her quite terrifying. Years later, Lyn was to become a very close and dear friend of ours and remains so to this day – but more on her later.

Jack swept into the room, a tall, tanned and dark-eyed man in his late 30s, with a hint of a Yorkshire accent. He whisked me out for coffee and told me his story.

To me, Jack was the Simon Cowell of the area; he knew everyone; he could be dressed in a tuxedo at a glamorous event; or be seen on his jet-skis, speeding through the waves of the Mediterranean with some gorgeous young man in tow. Later, Jack would marry a truly beautiful man, and sadly we have since lost touch.

Jack offered me a half-page in his newspaper every two weeks and, for several years, I would bring to the page famous faces and celebrity stories from those I had met, worked with or knew as friends that readers would recognise from back home. I had become a society page editor in Spain. I loved the opportunity to say to my UK clients, "Sorry, just need to take this call from my Editor in Spain."

Jack helped us enormously. He managed to stop the local telephone provider that had continued to take nearly 100 euros from us every month for seven months after we tried in vain to stop the direct debit, as we had no working telephone line anyway. He took us to meet his *Mama*, who made us the best spaghetti we had ever tasted while she regaled Jack with questions about his social life, like "why you don't bring a nice girl here to Mama?". Jack lived a colourful life and for many years it would be fun to meet him quite by chance while we were shopping in Benidorm – he always knew the best new bar to try. I loved the editorial meetings Jack and I used to have; there would always be a new coffee shop or restaurant to try, vital because, if we stayed in the office, everyone would need him for something.

I remember meeting him while we were showing one of our friends, Mark, around Benidorm. Jack appeared, resplendent in a brilliant white shirt, with a set of gleaming gnashers to match! Mark, a garrulous man by nature, was rooted to the spot while Jack tried to hurry us along to a gin and tonic bar. Mark could only stare, totally dumbstruck, like someone admiring a work of art! They did, in fact, strike up a platonic friendship (much to Mark's disappointment) and before long, Mark was flying out with his mate to join Jack for a drink while Jack gave them the lowdown on the best LGBT bars in town. What happens in Benidorm stays in Benidorm... that's all I know!

Around the same time, I contacted one of the local radio stations that we liked to tune into. I met the owners and, again with us media types, it's either instant love or instant hate. But we got on so very well. Like us, they were a husband and wife team, and they had worked hard and been part of the community for many years. I frequently appeared as an interviewee on their programmes and was delighted when they asked Bob and me to lunch. They suggested a fish restaurant by the sea and, in those days, I was too polite and not knowledgeable enough about the area to suggest anywhere else.

The problem is, I have a fatal allergy to fish. I worry that, one day, some little fish might think it amusing to get his revenge and take me with him to a fishy grave. I also have a slight heart murmur, so lifesaving injections are out of the question! So far, apart from a few visits to A&E, I had survived. I told Bob not to fuss and that when we got there, I would just have an omelette, and everything would be fine.

Sitting at a scrubbed wooden table, the shutters thrown back and the sun making sparkling dust rays before our eyes, I felt totally comfortable and safe in the knowledge that we were among new friends, and media friends at that. As we sipped after-lunch espresso, Bob began to fidget. I ignored this as I knew he needed a cigarette but, since our new friends were non-smokers, he was being polite at a cost to his withdrawal symptoms. Eventually Bob slid across the wooden bench where we were seated and said "Love, we need to get you home – you've gone polka dot!"

Oh no – the dreaded fish visitation had begun. We made our hasty goodbyes and promised to reciprocate soon, and Bob found somewhere in the hills not too far away for me to eject the contents of the omelette, which continued to swim out for another 12 hours.

Some months later, while shopping in Sainsbury's, I received an all-important call that could have changed our lives forever. I was asked to join the radio station as their main presenter.

Shocked, very humbled, and very honoured, I knew even without a chat with Bob that the answer had to be no. We were just not ready to commit to a full-time, grown-up life in Spain.

It did get us thinking, though, and when we were offered an opportunity to try it, we did!

In the early years of the millennium, air fares were still relatively cheap, and Bob and I considered whether we should take a step into working in the UK and in Spain on a two-week rota. Writing it now some years later I can see the folly in the words... but, we gave it a try.

The articles I wrote for the paper paid only a small amount of money, which was not at all a problem as they paid the electricity bill each month. However, a bigger commitment required a fuller strategy. Bob had received various offers of employment within marketing, and so we decided to pursue these avenues. Having chosen the best option, he had a meeting with the person concerned who offered him a tenth of his UK salary. The person, whom I shall call 'our client' was an expat who had been to Benidorm on her first holiday as a teenager and fallen in love with a local Spanish boy. The fairy-tale meeting resulted in marriage and, after working very hard, the couple had a family entertainment business, which was a flagship in Benidorm. Our client soon became a friend, and she and I shared a strong bond very quickly.

We soon realised that there was a great disparity between Spanish and British wages. After much deliberation, we decided that we would 'step off the cliff', and work two weeks in each country. Fortunately, Bob's UK employers were so keen for him to stay with the organisation that they agreed to his part-time two weeks on, two weeks off proposal. The hardest part was that I could not afford to join Bob on each of his trips as I had clients in the UK who needed me, so there would be some lonely nights for

Bob.

I distinctly remember being so excited to have booked a late flight on a Friday to join him, but, as the flight approached, I was feeling worse and worse with a bad cold. Still, when Friday rolled around, I was happy to be on the plane, soon to be home in our lovely cosy villa.

Bob met me at the airport carrying some yellow flowers and broke the news that one of our prospective clients needed to meet us for some advice, but assured me that it wouldn't take long. At 1am, still sitting under the stars in the grounds of a local restaurant, I felt the cocktail of cold and flu preparations, shaken and stirred with rioja, taking over... the client still in full flow... and then, I realised. This feeling was fish 'red alert' – my body was going into survival mode.

I interrupted the client's long story to politely ask, in a rather quivery voice, had she been absolutely sure that the dish she had told me was fish-free actually was fish-free. She had insisted so.

"Yes love, stop worrying," she sighed dramatically. "You are not in England now. It's Spain, there'll be no fish in it, just a bit of seafood, love."

We made another hasty retreat home where I collapsed, Bob just saving me from falling backwards on to the marble floor in our bedroom. Once again, I was lucky; the fish left its watery grave of my intestines and saved me from an earthier one.

It soon became clear after just three months of our two weeks on, two weeks off England/Spain schedule that it just did not work for us. Sadly, our client's husband, a Spaniard, could not seem to grasp that marketing and PR did not equal instant sales, so he decided to pay Bob only two-thirds of the agreed fee. But then, we were learning quickly that money in Spain never seems to be all that it seems.

We also learned very quickly that people who had made their money in Spain were unlikely to be good payers. It was such a shame as we really liked our client. The company would have had our unstinting loyalty, but we were also aware that in Spain that didn't seem to mean much either when it came to money! I still miss our client. I felt we lost a true friendship and I am sad our friendship did not survive.

So, Bob's foray into working in Spain was short-lived, and I was as happy to have him home as he was to be at home. But, as we all know, life often turns out as you least expect and, the following week, we were offered a corporate contract in the UK, meaning we would both be required to remain in the UK to work full-time for the foreseeable future.

It seems that Brits living in Spain are all lumped under the heading of 'expats', and yet they are not all couples who have re-tired and bought a place abroad to escape the winter and the arth-ritis. Each person has a story to tell, as I have indicated already. I have a very dear friend in England called Lynne, and it transpires that my dearest friend in Spain is called Lynn!

I mentioned her briefly earlier – she used to work for Jeff at the newspaper and, if the truth be known, I was a little in awe of her. Jeff obviously needed a right-hand person to manage all the stuff he didn't have time to do, and there was Lynn who was just SO efficient. We got to know one another via email first, and then through my visits to the office, and I soon became aware that, beyond that warm smile, she was the mother hen of the whole organisation.

'Spanish Lyn' is a wondrous woman of stories, anecdotes, information and knowledge. Her accounts of colourful ancestry kept us enthralled on many a New Year's Day when we would sit around the log fire in her beautiful *casa rustica*, replete from a long lunch of roasted meats, potatoes and vegetables together with hedgerow sauces and coulis.

As I have continued to be in awe of Lynn, I asked her to recount her story, in her own words, of her move to Spain in 1986.

Working with children was a great job. Although it was very stressful and tiring at times, and the rewards were few and far between, the odd young person who "made it" was worth all the heartache, aching joints, headaches and sleepless nights. Each year we took the children on "holiday", but we were becoming less and less successful at finding places to take such a large group and the stigma of "children in care" always rose its ugly head when I had to explain why the group was so large. Camping, in either tents and/or caravans, became the norm and I can honestly say the holidays always seemed a great success, but available places seemed less and less each year.

My boss had started a full-time course in January 1985 and, as his deputy, it fell on me to unofficially take charge, which I was reluctant to do. After ten years of being OIC (officer in charge), I took the job in Bristol as a deputy to ease off a bit, the ultimate responsibility falling on the boss rather than me. But extra shifts, meetings, staff rotas with 24/7 coverage, meant that if anyone didn´t turn up for work, I had to cover their shift after already working for 24 hours, which was exhausting.

March 1985, and I still had to somehow take a week's leave before the end of the financial year, otherwise I would lose it. My husband also worked with children in a special needs residential school as a teacher, which also included pastoral duties, i.e. sleeping over in the school at weekends to encourage hobbies, sports and outdoor activities. We were sometimes like ships that passed in the night, and both getting very tired with the situation.

We met at a travel agent on the Friday afternoon. He was already on school holidays, as it was very close to Easter, and my annual leave started the next day, the Saturday, so it was now or never. The agent only had three destinations available for the next day – out to Tenerife, which I thought too long a flight for just a week, or Malta, which we´d already visited, and lastly Benidorm. Eurgh… Benidorm?

Not much choice then, and I just wanted a quiet rest, to lie in a sunny place, sleep and read. Reports on Benidorm in the British press had not been encouraging and really, I was reluctant to commit. But we did, dashed to the cash point and withdrew the money. In those days, it being such a last-minute booking, cheques or credit cards were not accepted. We arrived home, threw a few things in a couple of suitcases and the following morning we were off, with many misgivings.

When we arrived, it was the Semana Santa, or Holy Week. The town was filled with Spanish families, lots of mums, dads and children, and quite delightful. I absolutely loved it. Not Benidorm as such, but the atmosphere was infectious and observing how everyone treated the children, coping with noisy, bad behaviour, screaming tantrums and what appeared, at first, as downright rudeness was to me, very impressive. I announced, to a very surprised husband, that this was where I wanted to live, not necessarily in Benidorm, but in Spain, where I felt as though I had "come home".

When we returned to the UK, we sat down and talked long and seriously about what we would do if we chose to eventually move to Spain. Because the country seemed very child-oriented, my plan was to open a holiday centre for all children, especially those with special needs, offering full-time, 24-hour care, with activities, cultural visits, but mainly "FUN", away from all the normal problems and restrictions of taking children on holiday in the UK. My husband said "OK" and gave me a year to come up with a do-able project, including daily routines/activities, menu, staffing, financial prospectus; but mainly how we would find our "guests", and where we would open the centre.

After a year in the planning, and contacts with three companies who specialised in "school" holidays, we seemed to be on the way. We booked a two-week holiday through a contact found in Dalton´s Weekly, who specialised in finding old houses with fenced-off land, the sort of space we needed to open our centre. Eventually we found what seemed to be the right spot, outside Benissa, costing around £15,000. The price was about right, so we made a contract with our "host", gave him a cheque for £5,000 as 33% deposit, and returned to the UK to further our plans for the move.

We sold the house, paid off the mortgage and prepared to move. My husband had to complete the summer term, Easter to the end of June, so, in the meantime, we bought a minibus, stocked it with everything we could think of, including tents and a porta-loo, as he and my 15 year-old nephew were going to camp on the land, working with the builders our original "host" had organised to complete the work for us, based on plans that had been drawn up. I had booked a couple of weeks' holiday in August and arrived with my niece, expecting to find six weeks' of work completed, the beginning of our centre rising from the dry countryside of Benissa.

Not so. When my husband and nephew arrived, they found that our "host" had not completed the purchase and had "dun a runner" with our money, as well as a lot of other people's hard-earned cash. I was devastated. £5,000 was a lot of money in 1986 but my husband, ever the optimist, suggested that we could perhaps buy another business and try to recoup the lost money. How would I fancy a bar?

I spent three days crying, not much fun for my niece and nephew, but I rallied a bit when we went into Altea, even though I was not impressed by the hot, dried-up landscape and dusty streets. After a meeting with an obnoxious guy who was handling the sale of a bar business, we decided OK, let's give it a try. In October 1986, we bought the traspaso to the little bar at La Cruz, in Altea.

Being non-drinkers, we were quite a novelty to the residents and, after a while, I got pretty fed up with the drunks, mainly the Brits and their behaviour, so I was usually sent home at midnight, earning me the name of Cenicienta, Cinderella in Spanish. I was always accompanied home and "protected" by one of our Spanish clients, usually Antonio, nicknamed "Tarzan" because of his prowess in yesso-ing between roof beams, who also lived on the same street as us in the old town, where we bought our first property. We were here to stay.

The bar was OK. We never recouped our losses, but it paid for everything we needed to live such as rent on our house, rent on the bar, the repayments on buying the business, food, utilities etc etc. But we both had spaces in our lives that had previously been filled with children.

As the sum in our bank account was not increasing, we decided to buy our first property with our dwindling resources, and my husband started a job in January 1987, teaching in an English school in Benidorm. In March, we were approached by a German couple we had got to know quite well, and they wanted to buy the bar business from us. This was fine by me as I was more or less running it on my own, although my husband worked evenings, and of course I was sent home at midnight, so he usually saw to the last clients and locked up.

Our lives together were not running that smoothly and even though I was quite happy, there was a big hole in my life. I announced to a shocked husband that I wanted a baby, preferably his. We´d been married for more than fourteen years and, throughout, had been involved with other people's children. Now I wanted one of my own.

We sold the bar at the end of March, bought our first house by the end of April. I celebrated my 40th birthday in the July and, by then, I was three months pregnant. My pregnancy was without a problem, I sailed through it, worked teaching English and, along with another two couples, bought the school where my husband was teaching.

He had been suffering from cancer since he was twenty-nine, when it was first diagnosed, plus three heart attacks from the stress of the treatment, and, although he´d been pretty cancer-free for most of our marriage, it raised its ugly head again, I´m sure, because of the stress caused by the many, unknown financial problems inherited when we bought the school. It also had a disastrous effect on our marriage. We eventually divorced, although we remained friends, and he became a distant but loving father to our son who was born in February 1988. He died in 2005, the day before his 65th birthday.

I bought the house in which my son and I now live in 1999, although we had lived there since October 1993 with a contract for "rental, with option to buy". Which I eventually did.

I have never regretted the decision to move my life to Spain, nor to raise my son alone since he was three years old. Yes, there have been hardships, and I´ve shed many tears, never having much money, but a better life than many. I could never imagine living anywhere else. I have not been disappointed by the Spanish way of life, the Spanish people I now consider my friends, nor that first inkling that I had "come home", back in 1985.

Many years ago, when I was studying at Southampton University, I had a very strange, and impressive, dream, which I relayed to my friend Jenny during a quiet moment in one of our lectures. I even drew it on the front of a folder when I was supposed to be taking notes. The scene was of an old, high stone wall with a large, old, arched doorway, with three-storey windows on either side. Metals bars covered them, and there were window boxes full of geraniums.

When my son was about three months old, I took a walk up the new steps to the old town just past my house, along the cobbled streets and into a part of the old town of Altea that I had never seen before. I had come upon the Glorieta, the scene of my dream many years ago, so easily recognisable. To say the hairs stood up on my arms and neck is an understatement. But some genetic memory, perhaps, had kicked in, perhaps I had been here before in a previous life. But I truly knew at that moment, I had come home.

Chapter 9:

Chapter 9

Little black bull & Fiestas

Life fell into a pattern where we would get away to our house in Spain whenever we could, and we enjoyed adding adornments to our Spanish nest. Many friends would come to visit, and we took pride in showing them the best tapas restaurants we had found, or the secret beaches that the tourists hadn't infiltrated. As we drove from Alicante airport, we would look out for that first black bull by the side of the motorway and eagerly point him out.

As I mentioned earlier, the massive black bull sign that I saw as I sleepily looked out of the window on my way to our new life as holiday home owners was the Osborne bull. That first sighting is forever emblazoned on my mind. Bob and I continued to point them out to each other whenever we saw them, but our favourite has remained the one seen on the A7 near Villajoyosa and Benidorm on that first fateful drive.

I am sure many fabulous people were born in 1956, however, it was also the year that the iconic, beautiful black bull was born. The black silhouette was created for the Osborne sherry company's Veterano brandy by the artist Manolo Prieto and must be one of the best marketing symbols ever designed. I put it right up there with Coca Cola and McDonald's.

About a year later, the first 'bullboard' (get it? Billboard... bullboard?) appeared on a major road in Spain, and many others followed. The Osborne bull, or 'Black Bully' as Bob and I affectionately named him, is a big boy! He weighs around 4,000 kilos and is over 14 metres in height.

In 1988, poor Black Bully was nearly forced into extinction when a new law prohibited any advertising to appear on public highways. With a threat of extinction, the court ruled that all the black bulls, all around Spain, should be removed. But thankfully, due to a public outcry that reached the Supreme Court, the bull was pardoned!

The judgement was allowed because it was said that the Osborne Bull had "exceeded its initial advertising sense and had been integrated into the landscape", although any wording about alcohol, or its brand name, had to be removed. The Osborne Group has sole rights to this day and the Osborne Bull remains their trademark. Long may our 'Black Bully' remain on the Spanish hillsides.

There was, however, a little cull and the 500 bulls now number around 90, still standing strong and proud! They are in fact much stronger than the first *toros*, which were made of wood, but the unrelenting extremes of weather took their toll and they are now made from metal. If you look at that back of the bull as you drive past, you will see he is supported by what looks like an enormous fence.

It is an understatement to report that there are many fiestas in Spain. I believe that fiestas define the Spanish mentality – even business life appears to be built around fiestas! And why not?!

The fiestas keep Spanish traditions alive and each of the local fiestas, of which there are many, ensure that local history and cultures endure, strengthening the fabric of the community. Many of the fiestas are religious celebrations due to Spain's strong Catholic tradition. Some fiestas are even adopted from pagan festivals, and some are wine-themed, popular in areas where the grape is grown.

Bob and I have witnessed many a fiesta; some we have embraced and enjoyed but others, like when we would just like to cross the road, buy a loaf of bread, go to the bank or worst, eat out, but all the restaurants are closed, have been, admittedly, a source of frustration. That said, the fiesta is a social vehicle for strengthening community bonds and having a great deal of fun.

Good weather is almost guaranteed, so even the oldest residents are able to attend. In fact, it is a right, and no-one would expect the *abuelos*, the grandparents, to be left at home when, instead, they can have a younger family member carry their favourite armchair out on to the pavement so they can watch the procession and celebrations in comfort. Fiestas take place all year, even in the depths of winter and in the southern areas of Spain it is, at least usually, still warm enough.

In the area where we were, like the rest of Spain, New Year's Eve was a big event and will continue to be in perpetuity, I have no doubt. *Noche Vieja* necessitates many, many preparations. Lots of family get-togethers are the norm; from great-grannies to the youngest great-grandchild, all are expected to attend a big feast, often with friends and extended family in attendance. In the very rural villages of Spain over this period, most families grow their own vegetables, and rear their own chickens and pigs. Besides the joints of pork, they make their own sausages, *morcilla* (blood sausage) and chorizo. Suckling pig and wild boar are a speciality, certainly in the northern villages around Léon, as are various game birds in the hunting season.

In the old church square in our neighbouring Altea La Vella, it seemed the whole village was waiting for the 12 dongs of midnight to eat their grapes, one for each peel of the chimes, in order for good luck to enter everyone's lives in the following year. And, of course, to ensure even more good luck, one must wear red underwear!

Our favourite family ritual, whether Bob and I were on our own, or with Hayley and Sean, was to stand on our roof terrace, flutes of bubbles in hand, and watch from our 360-degree vista as each town and village set off their fireworks at the stroke of midnight. Then, just a few minutes later, over the headland, we could watch the light show from Benidorm's fireworks, reaching so far into the New Year's sky that we were still able to enjoy them, but from a much quieter, more homely setting.

Hard on its heels comes, of course, the *Fiesta de los Reyes*, when the three kings arrive from the beaches to bestow sweets to the children in the streets. Three Kings Day is always on 6 January, but the national holiday starts from dusk on 5 January and all eateries close. The last to close are the *panaderías*, selling their *Roscón de Reyes*, the Three Kings Cake. The first time we tried the cake was with our friend Lynn who explained, as I nearly choked on something in the cake, that I had found the small prize hidden inside by the baker, and that I was to be crowned Queen for the day. Bob was not as lucky, as he bit on the other hidden treasure in the cake – a bean, which meant the purchase of next year's *Roscón* was on him!

We have always made it a rule to travel and stay in a different Spanish town or city for 5 January, as, to us, it is an absolute phenomenon; our travels to Costa de la Luz, Andalusia and Northern Spain demonstrate that anyone that is able to take to the streets does so. The noise is unbelievable, like being part of a huge festival, and again we marvel at how much the respective mayors spend on the event for their people. There are light shows, huge stages erected hosting anything from choirs, to flamenco, to bands or orchestras and, of course, the kings make their parade (*la cabalgata*). We have also learnt to eat at midday on the 5th, as otherwise we would have to go hungry until 7 January - even the hotels are not keen on room service at this time of year.

Opinions differ across the country as to whether Santa Claus (*Papá Noel*) is displacing the traditions of the Three Kings. Having experienced Christmas Eve in many areas across the country, I do not believe that the Three Kings will be usurped from their esteemed position any time soon. Christmas Eve in this Catholic country, from dusk onwards, brings forth families and friends to worship, many walking through the streets with candles, singing hymns. The churches are filled to the brim, and so are the shops, which stay open late. And, miraculously, you can find somewhere to eat! So, I believe that the two holidays work very nicely together in Spain.

Fiestas abound for the rest of the year, too. I believe it would be impossible to catalogue every one, as they differ from region to region, town, city, village, street to street. The time of year can differ right across the twelve months of the year – hence the problems we have experienced regarding doing business in Spain...!

In March, there is a well-known fiesta held in most towns and villages within the Valencian *Communidad,* and, as Benidorm sits within it, Las Fallas is a big event. Each year in the week leading up to 19 March, the most beautiful and often surreal paper effigies are erected. They are displayed in the streets and then, on the 19 March, they are taken to the beach and burnt. Weeks of artwork are consumed by flames, but everyone has had fun.

Easter, *Semana Santa,* follows on Fallas' heels but, apart from the religious holidays, it isn't such a momentous event for Benidorm apart from it is the beginning of many thousands of Spanish holidaymakers flocking to the town. In Andalusia, Easter is big business; in Seville, one of our most favourite cities, the *Semana Santa* processions are world-famous. The main features are the life-sized sculptures of Christ and creepy-looking hooded penitents; obviously this procession has happened for centuries but, in later years, the penitents' costume was sadly adopted by the Ku Klux Klan. Two weeks later, the *Fería de Abril* festivities arrive. In recent years, Benidorm has welcomed Seville's *Fería de Abril* tradition, and now many Benidorm bars and restaurants embrace the traditional foods and drinks of Andalusia, with flamenco music and dancing.

June sees the next big 'do' right across Spain, the *Fiesta de San Juan.* The eve of St John the Baptist is beach party night. It is not unusual to see many Spaniards jumping over beach campfires, throwing euro coins into the sea together with candles. These days, as there are strict safety laws, you won't see campfires in Benidorm, but perhaps on the more secluded little-known beaches.

It is impossible to ignore the summer fiestas involving bulls and bull-running. Personally, I abhor them, and continue to steer clear of them. Certainly, while we lived in the Costa Blanca, we would avoid the Dénia or Javea fiestas. Not that these were, by any stretch of the imagination, the only ones involving bulls. Men of all ages in many villages would be trying their luck at side-stepping a bull and thinking themselves even more courageous by doing so if one of their friends had set the bull's horns alight. I'll say no more.

Benidorm Pride is in its first decade, and every year it happily goes from strength to strength. The streets are adorned with rainbows flags for nearly a week during September.

The end of summer brings a further round of fiestas, like La Tomatina, billed as 'The World's Biggest Food Fight.' Held in the town of Buñol near Valencia, many thousands of people join the throng who, basically, throw more than one hundred metric tons of tomatoes at one another. Buñol normally has a population of around 9,000 inhabitants but, like the tomatoes, this number swells to around 50,000 during the fiesta time. It was lovely to see a few years ago that even Google honoured the 70th year of La Tomatina for a day on their homepage.

Perhaps one of the most famous and bizarre fiestas are the Tarragona *castells*, Tarragona's spectacular human tower festival. As many as 30 'human tower' groups battle it out to be chosen as the most complex human tower structure. The *castells* have been awarded the UNESCO Intangible Cultural Heritage of humanity designation.

In Barcelona, the biggest party of the year has taken place each year since 1902, known as *Fiesta la Mercè*, and embodies the chance to say goodbye to summer and welcome in the hues of autumn. The fiesta lasts for about five days and is held in honour of the Mare de Déu de la Mercè, Our Lady of Mercy. Around two million revellers join in the many events and street fiesta – they even have their own human towers here, too.

The month of November was Benidorm's choice for its town fiesta, and many thousands of Brits now join in the fun. The fiesta begins during the second week of November, and the fancy dress and floats parade has become legendary, as well as the fireworks, all components of a fab fiesta. My personal favourite part is the lesser-known Artichoke fiesta, the *Festa de la Carxofa*, which takes place the third week in November in Benidorm Old Town. The fiesta is a thanksgiving for the harvest and, although it stopped during the Spanish Civil War, it was reinstated in the 70s. The fiesta takes place over three days where, sometimes, free food and drink is offered by some Old Town establishments. It culminates with a burning of the artichoke in Constitution Square.

I would never, ever try and hazard a guess at just how many fiestas take place in Spain. From the millions taking part in Spain's biggest religious pilgrimage, which descends on the little town El Rocío in southern Spain around May time, right through to the small town of Ibi where, on the last Sunday of December, the *Día de los Innocentes*, 'the floured ones', *els enfarinats*, dress in military gear and throw flour, eggs and fire crackers – I did warn you that, in Spain, fiestas abound!

Chapter 10:

Disability

In 2007, I had the misfortune of experiencing Costa Blanca beach life from the seat of a wheelchair. This was long before the days of the TV programme *Benidorm* and the show's formidable Madge and her mobility scooter!

During our 'big contract' in the UK, I decided to hold a 70s night and was delighted when my client agreed to a Summer Nights themed event. I was doubly delighted when the well-known presenter and DJ, the lovely David Hamilton, agreed to join us and be our star host for the evening. I am so happy to read, as I write this, that David is still very much out there, currently on a cruise liner, keeping peoples' memories of their rock n roll days alive.

I had meticulously planned the event, apart from the rental of an all-important dancefloor, which my client had decided would make a fitting addition to the celebrations. When the colour-changing, really rather raised, dancefloor was in place, I commented that, while it was lovely, its height was somewhat dangerous, and that someone might fall off it...

The night was a great success, and no-one fell off the dance floor. I, however, tripped while stepping up on to it. After a painful night, Bob took me to A&E in Bangor the next morning, propping me up along a wall while he parked the car as there were no seats outside. I was unceremoniously plonked in a wheelchair and wheeled to the end of a row of seats in the waiting room, where everyone had to pass me, knocking my foot. Finally, following an X-ray, I was taken into a room to meet with a doctor who had the best ever cure for making people feel rapidly better. He took my hand in his and said, "I have some very bad news for you." My immediate thought was that I would never walk again!

He then continued, "You have broken your ankle and your fifth metatarsal."

With a sigh I thanked him and said, "Phew! Is that all?!"

I had a dayglo pink cast fitted and, with the help of my Bob, managed to carry on as normal. Well almost – no one tells you that the cast is so heavy that you frequently keel over! Or that you can't sleep in a comfortable position, or that you must set off to the loo before you even need to go. I was, however, a model patient, and managed to make the local newspaper who asked "a PR Guru in a wheelchair? Has she fallen from her client's sky-high heels?" At the time, one of my clients owned a designer shoe shop and, to my embarrassment, I had to admit that the deed had been done while wearing a pair of chain store sandals and *not* some gorgeous designer Cinderella slippers. Perhaps, in order to maintain a famous shoe designer's reputation, that was actually the best possible outcome.

We had booked our month's holiday to Spain before I had my accident and it was a nail-biting week as we awaited my appointment with the consultant the day before our flight was due to leave. Luckily, we received his agreement that I could fly, and the cast came off the day before our flight. Again, I knew so little, like the fact that a cast doesn't just come off and you can put your shoe on... no, I still couldn't walk, and was wheelchair-bound for another six weeks. Hastily we made calls to the airline and Bob so gallantly sorted it all out for me – we were off to our *casa* as planned!

The morning of our flight was adrenaline-filled as Bob's brother, Dave, dropped us off at Manchester Airport. Bob pushed me up to the check-in desk and, at that moment, I realised that Dave had driven off with my crutches, making it was impossible for me to get out of the chair. At that point, we regretted lecturing Dave about road safety and the fact he must never, ever look at a text or take a phone call while driving (this was before the very sensible and much-needed law became statute). Fortunately, Dave checked his phone on reaching home, and we waited, along with a very patient airport accessibility person, for Dave to return with my crutches.

As we were in mid-summer season, there were several of us passengers who were categorised as disabled that day. The poor accessibility person had so many people to meet and get into the small lift down to airside that, in the end, Bob offered to help. I wish we had a photo of Bob pushing me along in my wheelchair with one hand and another person's chair in the other, together with a gentleman with limited vision holding on to Bob's shoulder and a lady with a white stick holding his other arm… bless my Bob!

Spain in August can see the scolding rays reach 45°C, and poor Bob soon found that pushing me, even though I am only a size 10, and a picnic basket, up even the slightest incline was very hot work! The easiest of rituals became arduous. As you know, visiting a hypermarket has always been something of a double-edged sword for us; we love the fact that the girls are swishing around on skates, but hate the fact that next to stands selling watches, others are selling puppies in glass boxes. However, negotiating a toilet door with supposed disability access was nearly the end of me!

Bob wheeled me to the ladies' toilets, and I managed to propel myself inside. The problem was that the disabled toilet was at the end of the room, and fitted with a sliding door on a slight incline, so there was no chance of me getting into the cubicle – and, I suspect, even less of me ever getting out. Tena Lady had to rule the day!

It was car parking at one of the fast food restaurants that was our most taxing manoeuvre, though. There was a slope from the disabled spot to the door of the restaurant – but a huge bush had been planted in the middle of the slope. That one proved too much, even for us! One day while seated at a roadside café – much easier to get to – an elderly man walked by with his dog. The dog and I locked eyes; he had a white cast covering his front right leg, and he hobbled over to me, sat down, and rested his head on my pink cast. What a photo it would have made, although we will never forget it.

We took to venturing out after 2pm when the sun was slightly less virulent. The first hurdle was getting on to a beach. There would be a sign depicting disability access, but there would inevitably be steps! So, Bob would load me, the chair and our picnic back into the car and drive off to another beach. Eventually, we found a beach with a slope down to a boardwalk – hurrah! I longed to slip out of my chair and slide myself on my bottom to the water's edge and dip my poor broken bones into the Med. By now, all Bob wanted to do was collapse on the sand!

Our joy was short-lived. As Bob rattled the wheelchair along the temporary wooden slats to the sea, a lifeguard began to roll in the other end of the boardwalk at a rate of knots. Bob began to run, me resembling a rag doll as I was thrown from one side of the chair to the other, my straw hat bobbing along, me gripping onto the picnic basket for dear life!

"Stop! Stop!" we shouted.

"¡Está cerrado!" he shouted back. "¡Siesta!" So, obviously the beach had a siesta too, and disabled people were not allowed on the beaches at that time. Eventually, though, my British Bulldog Bob won, and the beach guy gave up and walked off, muttering to himself and shrugging his shoulders.

I already had my bikini on and, in no time, I had whipped off my cotton dress and slid on to the sand ready to navigate my way to the water's edge. But from the lofty heights of my wheelchair I had no idea of the burning sand that awaited my bikinied bottom, and I must have resembled roadrunner as I shuffled along the sand quicker than any centipede would have!

I have held a Blue Badge for some fifteen years, which is, of course, as I write, a European Blue Badge. In many ways, over the past fourteen years of our time living in Spain, Bob, as principal driver, and I have seen a huge move forward in disability access. There is one problem which, for me, even when visiting Spain without the wheelchair, has been a constant – the pole displaying the disabled parking signs! The pole appears on the pavement, close to the road, and in such a position that the passenger door cannot be opened more than six inches - even for my small frame, it's difficult to get out. It is not so bad now that I am able to walk, but it was impossible during my wheelchair days. This would obviously be the same for any car passenger with disabilities. Bob and I established a system, which we called our car parking fandango; Bob finds the space and pulls up behind it; he gets me out of the car; he gets back in the car; and drives into the space. On our return, he drives out of the space, so I can get in. This is not without its difficulties as, within split seconds of said manoeuvring, a scooter or motorbike might appear and take a part of the parking space, so the manoeuvre is thwarted and aborted.

Another problem is the 'she doesn't look disabled' argument. This happens when another driver spots the space and nips into it, and when Bob peeps the horn to point out that we were in the middle of parking, the abuse begins – "my husband/wife is more disabled than yours!" On one occasion in our neighbouring town of Alfaz del Pi, I stood in the parking space while Bob was straightening up the car to drive in and a German 'gentleman' nipped in front of him and, even when he saw me standing in the space, he didn't stop. I had to throw myself out of the way. And yes, of course his comment was "See! She is not disabled, she can jump!" Oh dear… I have brittle bones, might I add.

I am pleased to say that, over the years, the various Mayors of the many towns and cities have realised that the 'Disabled Euro' is worth a lot to the economy and so with that, and European regulations in place, beaches and supermarkets have become more accessible. Although, in our experience, the roadside disabled parking signs might be the last to go!

Chapter 11:

Driving in Spain

Most people planning a day out on holiday might arise around 8am, have breakfast, pack up the car, drive around the corner, forget something, drive back to the house, answer a call of nature, pick up the forgotten picnic bag/mother-in-law, and set off.

By now its 10am, and the chosen destination is two hours' drive away. At midday, they arrive at the tourist destination of their choice, where the driver will spend an hour finding a parking space. This is not because there aren't any or because the driver and passengers haven't brought a map (if they don't have GPS) – in many parts of Spain, it's more likely to be because the Mayor has chosen to mark street names in a language other than Castilian Spanish, for instance Basque, Catalan, Valencian etc so that, if your map is not in the chosen language, the street signs will not correspond with anything on your map!

Eventually, you might stop and decide to have a browse around the shops. But, oh no – the shops are closed! The museum you were hoping to visit is also closed. Having located a tourist information office on one of the street signs, you head there in search of advice... but oh no! The tourist office is closed until 6pm. Knowing you have to start your journey back around 4pm, it means all you can do now is go and find a restaurant, which will undoubtedly be lovely but, after that, still nowhere is likely to be open. So, it will be back in the car and homeward bound. So much for your day out! Perhaps it's a clever ruse by the tourist boards - who knows? But I doubt it.

Bob and I learned all this the hard way and, in the later

years, we would book an overnight stay in a hotel, as it was the only way for us to enjoy a town or city and see it when things were open!

Having travelled the length and breadth of this dramatic country, I must say it is worth every moment of frustration one might encounter. A country so big – to us in the UK, anyway – that we have experienced Christmas Day in the snow in the fabulous capital of Madrid, and, just days later, sunbathed in Jerez. We have found the roads in Spain to be fabulous, the saloon-style hostelries along the main roads and across the mountains offering an unbelievably warm welcome, and providing tapas, main meals, provisions and artisan gifts – even a bed for the night. Each time we returned home to the potholes of the North of England, we eulogised about the Spanish roads and motorways.

Driving in Spain takes some getting used to, and not just because of driving on the opposite side of the road. There are many rules which must be obeyed, and which one will not find in the Spanish Highway Code. I do, however, love listening to an elderly friend of ours who was born in a remote village past Lorca. He tells of the 'odd and even days', where on one day of the week you parked on the odd-numbers side of the main street, and the next you parked on the evens side of street and so on – at least there was conformity!

Another fact we have found interesting is that the Spanish have found their horns! Not on animals, but in their cars. When we first moved to Spain, we noticed the lack of them, and one of our friends told us that Spanish people treat a honking of a horn as a worse insult than that of the middle finger variety – but, certainly over the last six years or so, things have changed. They are still not used for alerting fellow drivers or pedestrians of road safety, but rather to herald a big win by the local or national football team, or if there is a female to whom they wish to show their appreciation. The best one is for greeting friends, because this comes with the car actually stopping, and a conversation being held in the middle of a main road. Whilst this may cause Bob to make use of his horn, the friends will look at us askance, hurt, even, then shake their heads in wonderment and then carry on talking.

Certainly, in the area where we live it amazes us that Spanish pedestrians are so sure that a car will stop for them on a pedestrian crossing that they step out at any moment they fancy. And the cars do stop, every time! I do worry that, as more UK people buy property in Spain, this might be a problem for both sides as, of course, in the UK we only have to stop at a pedestrian crossing or at traffic lights if it is safe to do so; as we all know, that means we are rarely prepared to stop at a split-second's notice for random pedestrians and, for the uninitiated, new to driving in Spain, they might be surprised to find a Spaniard on their bonnet. Although, contrarily, pedestrian crossings also appear to make good places to park across, too!

I do find the double-parking endearing. I do not know why I do find it so, or why they do it. We often go to eat out in Albir, where there are many restaurants, and so parking near to them is usually difficult in the summer months. Double-parking happens so often. The car drives up, double-parks, hazard lights on, two well-dressed people exit the car and go into a close-by restaurant. If your car is the one alongside the double parker, please don't sit there honking your horn and expecting someone to come and move their car; remember that car horns are for situations such as greeting friends, or showing admiration of a shapely leg, etc.

As the passenger, roundabouts terrify me. Obviously, when Bob is driving around a roundabout, I am the one locking eyes with the driver who plans to join the roundabout while choosing not to slow or stop to give way to traffic, but just joins it regardless. In fairness, there are no white lines to indicate that stopping is required before joining. We have canvassed many of our friends, both Spanish and expats, on this subject and the best piece of advice given was this; "As no one knows which lane you should use to leave or join, it's a free for all – so just go for it!"

Chapter 12:
Business in Spain – Siesta time!

Throughout the years we owned our dream home in Spain, the siesta became something of a bugbear to us.

Spanish artists and famous intellectuals such as Salvador Dali and Camilo José Cela were great defenders of the siesta, which Cela described as "Iberian yoga". I understand that Spain is not the only country where its citizens like a nap after lunch and that, in China, it is a constitutional right to have a rest at midday, while Japan has 'nap salons', and the Bangladeshis have *bhat-ghum*, their 'rice sleep'. And so a form of siesta is to be found around the world, especially where there has been an historic Spanish influence. I have spent a lot of time in Paris and other areas of France and yes, the French enjoy a leisurely lunch, but they do manage to get back to work and function in the late afternoon (no quips concerning our French cousins and romantic interludes in the afternoon, please).

I don't mean to be rude (which of course means that I am about to be rude), but how can they do it? How can a whole country shut at 2pm and not open until after 5pm?

I can understand that workers in the fields had to, and continue to need to, start early in the morning, resting during the searing heat of the middle of the day before recommencing at 6pm, BUT, if you work in a bank, WHY do you drive in your air-conditioned car to your air-conditioned office only to stop work at 1pm, drive home to eat your meal, have a snooze then drive back and start again? While all of these people are having a little siesta, the rest of the world is tearing its hair out trying to elicit an email or a telephone response from Spain.

Endeavouring to pay a bill is a nightmare. Having finally succumbed to online banking, which has been a Godsend, some bills are still required to be paid at the bank. The counters are high, so the customer must resemble a meerkat to the cashier, and could be one of the reasons why the cashiers always look so shocked when you have to peer over the counter to talk to them. After the pleasantries of *buenos días/buenas tardes*, the dance will commence:

"May we pay this bill, please?

"Es... No."

"Why can't we pay the bill?"

"Es not possible."

"Why is it not possible? We have money in our account!"

"Today is not a day that the bank gives you to pay bills."

"Why?"

"Es now 11.30 am on Thursday. All bills must be paid by 11am on Thursday."

"But when we came in the time was 10am."

"Yes, *sí*, you may pay it then but not now."

"OK, can we pay it tomorrow?"

"No, it is not possible."

"Can we pay it Monday?"

"Es not possible because it is our fiesta."

"In all of Spain?"

"No, here on this calle, this street... *gracias, adiós.*"

On another occasion, we decided to move some money from our savings account to our current account, both held at the same bank. In fact, we didn't have a savings account; we had a life endowment account, which the cashier opened some years before for us when we asked for a simple savings account, but he decided otherwise, and didn't bother to tell us. When I asked why he had done this, he said "es better for you". Because it was an endowment account, it of course took longer to withdraw money. On an occasion when we were staying in Spain for three weeks, we decided to move some 'just in case' money over from our endowment account, otherwise known to us as our 'not-a-savings' account, into our current account. We waited in the pre-requisite long queue for nearly an hour, and when we finally took up our meerkat position, we requested that 600 euros be moved from our endowment account to our current. There was much bashing of keyboard keys and clicking of the mouse until at last the printer made a loud noise and a piece of thick paper was stamped with great gusto and Bob was told, "here, you name please". We thanked the cashier and, because I have learned to check and check again, I checked our bank statement, and 600 euros had been taken out of our current account and put into the endowment – the opposite of what we had wanted. So, we queued again, we retook our meerkat positions, and I explained the error. The senior cashier was called, the manager was called, there was much bashing of keys and clicking and head-scratching and then the printer made a loud noise, which spewed out a piece of paper that was then stamped to within an inch of its life. The subsequent conversation went something like this:

Me: When will the money be back in our current account, as our mortgage is due out of it tomorrow?

Cashier: This will take many days.

Me: But we will be overdrawn in our current account because of your mistake.

Cashier: Yes, this will happen, and many charges will happen also.

Me: But our mortgage is with this bank, so can you not explain the mistake to them?

Cashier: It is not possible because you sign your contract and say you will pay your mortgage every month.

Me: OK... well what can I do?

Cashier: You must always pay on time.

Me: Right... can we come in next week and see your Manager?

Cashier: Next week is fiesta, so es not possible.

And with that, the Meerkats left the building!

One area, however, where we find this famous international tradition benefits us is on the beach. We can leave our watches at home on the days we are heading to the wonderful white sands of the Costa Blanca, and not just to save them from being ruined in the sand. No, it is the fact that, just before 2pm, Spanish mamas and papas round up their children, dry them off in a towel, close the beach umbrella, get Grandma out of the beach chair and hey presto, off they go, and leave the beach! Cecil B. DeMille would have loved them as extras for his famous *Ten Commandments* film, hordes of them tramping across the hot sand towards their cars or hotels. If it gets to about 2.15pm, the pace quickens, and faces become more determined as lunch and nap MUST be enjoyed at this time, lest the tradition pass unobserved, tipping the earth from its axis.

Chapter 13:

Selling Casa de Sueños

Around year six of our 'buyer beware' Spanish home ownership, we decided that, as much as we loved the house, we were bored and wanted to sell. The Spanish 'crisis' had hit, the recession had hit the UK, and the exchange rate had worsened, making the mortgage a problem, while house prices had plummeted, and we were finding it more and more expensive to 'nip over' – so we felt that the time had come.

Sadly, the universe did not agree with us and so, unbeknownst to us at the time, we had many more years of casa ownership ahead of us. I believe that the universe will always take care of us, and so was philosophical about selling, which was just as well. Many people suggested that we 'long let' but we loved our casa, and we had made it so beautiful. We had also heard so many horror stories of seemingly lovely tenants becoming squatters, or worse.

One of our friends had rented his house out to, what appeared to be, a perfect couple. They were quiet and always paid on time, having the rent money to hand for our erstwhile friend whenever he knocked on the door. It was only when they left one day in the dead of night that our friends found thick soil smeared into the floor tiles, and remnants of a cannabis crop in every room.

For our first foray into selling our property, we decided on a well-known Spain-based estate agency that sold mainly to Brits. We made an appointment and duly turned up at the modern offices, all floor-to-ceiling windows and brightly coloured pictures of perfect haciendas. The doors were shut and bolted, not an unusual occurrence towards siesta time – but then it was still very much closed on our subsequent visits. It turned out that the bottom had truly fallen out of the market and was languishing somewhere in the depths of the azure Mediterranean Sea. We had already missed the boat!

Undaunted, we chose a Spanish firm and, after our attempts to speak Valencian, and with much gesticulation and pointing at watches, we understood that we had made an appointment for noon the next day at our house. A lady arrived not much after the agreed time. She tripped around the house in her high heels, sat herself down in our lounge and proceeded to waft a contract and a pen under my nose, obviously wishing me to sign the tri-coloured set of papers. I was about to, when I asked her in my best Spanish why there was a figure of twenty-five percent mentioned. "*Comisión!*" she barked, "*Firma aquí!*" Well, I was not about to "sign here" and commit to twenty-five percent commission! She was not a happy bunny and left shortly after I told her "*de ninguna mañera, José!*" – "No way, José!"

We decided to take matters into our own hands; after all, we owned a PR business, so why not utilise our PR skills to sell our house? I took a photo of our casa and worked on making our leaflet look enticing to anyone who might want to consider buying. We also wrote the details in Spanish, English and German, just to be on the safe side. We drove around the other *urbanizaciones*, or housing estates, within a six-kilometre radius, delivering out leaflets – and then I had the brainwave to put a leaflet on every car windscreen at our local Sunday *rastro*, the fabulous market I have already eulogised about, where, from 8am, anything from fur coats, to boats, to animals, to bikes could be purchased at a bartered price. Thankfully our dear friend Lynn, once more to our rescue, saw what we were doing and advised us that in Spain this was against the law! We could do nothing more than retrace our steps, now in the heat of the midday sun, and remove them all.

We visited all the local restaurants and asked if they would kindly display our leaflets which they did, but since the owners all had that certain look in their eye of 'you want me to do this for free?', it cost us quite a lot of euros in tips.

I had met a very lovely man who happened to be a medium, and who is well-known not just in the area where we were, but across Europe. He was so supportive of us and especially of my undaunted ideas for selling our house, but it was obvious when I consulted him that it was not going to sell soon. He couldn't give me an untrue answer, but my mum or dad would come through to him and it made my visits to him all the more precious.

I investigated raffling the house, but if we didn't get two hundred thousand people to buy a ticket then it was no use, and there was the small matter that we didn't actually own it – the bank owned half of it and, as we paid the mortgage to them, they would most likely refuse to agree to it.

Once again, our ever-faithful friend Lynn tried some online sites for us, and she was kind enough to shield us from some of the offers that she received, such as someone wanting to 'try it out' by living in it for free for a month, and other offers such as taking her to dinner. Wisely, Lynn accepted none of these!

We approached our bank and asked them if our mortgage could be re-negotiated, as we had been told by our Spanish accountant that our mortgage was 'toxic' – buying in such haste (if you remember, we had only 15 mins in the bank when we bought our house), we had agreed to pay a high rate of interest. We were not surprised to be told, "No, no change, es not possible!"

We found a Brit estate agent, but he kept forgetting to close our windows so we either had flies greeting us when we returned home or, if it had rained, our curtains were wet.

Finally, we found a Brit estate agent that had been in the business, and in Spain, for many years – and what a great guy he turned out to be. He and his wife became friends of ours, and we would always call on them when we were in Spain. He told us it would be a long haul, that we wanted too much money for it, and that we should rent it out. We heeded some of his wise words and, for a very short time, even contemplated renting it out. Around year nine, we relented slightly and agreed to meet a couple who would like to rent with a view to buy. Our stipulation was non-smokers and no pets. The couple turned up at our gate with a dog and smelling strongly of tobacco (not the dog, obviously, although I do think the nicotine had stuck to his lovely coat too). The 'non-smoking' couple told us that the dog would not be staying in the house... we declined the offer of their rental and decided it was sell or bust.

Our estate agent was kindness itself, and often took people around our house when we were in the UK. There were various humorous stories, like the guy who really liked our house and came around with his elderly mother and father, and it was in our lounge that said mother told said son that the house was too small, because mother had decided that morning that she and Dad should move in with their son. Apparently the son looked like he was about to burst into tears, and they left very quickly.

We had the couple who complained that they hadn't wanted 'rustic'... our house was 20 years old! There was the dentist who was going to leave her husband and buy our house – but could we wait a year because she hadn't told her husband yet?

We decided that the house would sell when it decided it wanted to be sold. In the meantime, we would make the most of our base and cover as much of the gigantic, beautiful country of Spain as was humanly possible – and that is exactly what we did. Wherever we travelled, we always ensured that, especially during the winter months, we left a couple of days before returning home to enjoy a stay at our casa and make at least one visit to Benidorm. Apart from the people-watching, we loved the shoe shops, where we would both find next season's gorgeous shoes at ridiculously low prices.

Benidorm is often known as the 'snowbird' destination and, thankfully for many, the hen and stag parties have moved on with the attraction of cheap flights opening up more of Europe. The snowbirds, the white-haired pensioners who take advantage of two-or-three-month-long all-inclusive deals to escape the harsh winters and damp conditions causing their ailments, aren't only British, either – although they tend to be the longest roosters, the Spanish pensioners also enjoy "a bit of Beni". They are allowed a two-week free holiday per year by their government, and Benidorm is often the resort of choice. The two distinct groups are easily differentiated. Our sun-loving Brits of 60+ can most likely be found around the 'Brit' end of Benidorm, near to Levante Beach, while the Spaniards tend to stay around the Plaça del Castell, right on the headland of the Old Town. From this vista, the beauty of the two famous white beaches can be observed; Levante to the east and Poniente to the west. The Spanish snowbirds do venture down along the sea front of Levante, but one has the feeling that it is mainly to observe the English ones. While both sets of folk wear sunglasses, that appears to be where the similarity ends. The Spanish will be well-dressed, men in their shirts and V-neck pullovers, carrying a coat, and the women in their sludge-coloured anoraks, smartly dressed in boots and scarves. Meanwhile, our female white-haired lovelies are in white cropped shorts with sandals and bright toenails, a boob tube, and sporting a red crepe-paper décolletage, while the men will be in white shorts, sandals with socks, and a polo shirt. Bless them! As most Brits have paid for all-inclusive, they quite rightly make the most of it, and return to the 'digs' for their lunch, while the Spaniards are more likely to be found in Tapas Alley, eating fresh fish and seafood by the shed load. Their lunchtimes are noisy social affairs, and you could never imagine that they would fit in (or wish to for one moment) in one of our seaside towns during the winter in a dining room at a quiet guest house. Well, good luck to them! I have not left the Scandinavian population out on purpose; it's harder to differentiate between their expats and their holiday makers, as most of each appear to spend their times on bicycles, looking super fit, lean and groomed.

While the all-inclusive hotel deal has brought more people to Benidorm, boosting hotel occupancy figures, it has had the opposite effect on the economy of restaurant owners, who rely especially on lunchtime trade, and who are no doubt very glad of the Spanish winter trade. In 2015, the Association of Bars, Restaurants and Cafes of Benidorm (ABRECA) said that consumer spending at local restaurants fell by 12 percent. Previously, clients would spend up to 22 euros per head, but now were spending only 15.

For me, winter in Benidorm is the best time; it's fun to walk along the promenade of Levante and decide which coffee, cake and brandy sign will entice us for our elevenses. We have a favourite, and we especially enjoy the winter brandy offer, as during the summer it appears to be much more, erm... watery! One must consider that the cost of such a sojourn is around two euros each, so who can blame them if the water jug tips a little towards the brandy in peak season!

It is untrue, however, that you barely hear a Spanish accent in Benidorm because while there are a great number of expat residents, it is also the major resort for internal tourism with Spain. Far from never hearing a Spanish accent, you can hear virtually every accent, dialect and language of Spain, and there are many!

Having recently visited the wondrous and fabulous Valencia, where one end of the street is in Valencian and the other is in Castilian Spanish, I am able to speak with some experience. In Catalonia, they speak Catalan, which is a little like Valencian, but, we are assured, they are *not* the same! In the Comunidad Valenciana, they don´t speak Catalan, but they do speak Valencian and Castilian Spanish.

Both Catalan and Valencian, as well as Galician and Basque, would have previously been considered, I believe, as *dialectos*, but some consider them as entirely separate languages. The arguments have endured for many years and will most likely continue to do so. From what I understand, Valencian is very similar, but not the same, as Catalan, and is spoken mainly in the Valencia region. The Valencians get upset by what they see as a takeover by the Catalans if their language is described as a dialect. Valencian predates Catalan, so how can Valencian be the same? Most unsuspecting tourists, having listened to their 'Learn Spanish in Five Days' CD will speak Castilian Spanish in these regions and upset everyone! One thing we have learned of Spain and the Spaniards is that there is never a straightforward answer, and there will be at least two different opinions on everything.

There are many beautiful valleys, mountain ranges, villages, towns and cities to visit in Spain, and there are people more blessed than I am to talk and write about them. The thrill of having a place in another country meant we could experience a completely different life, one that that you can't have at home. In the UK, we live in what is fast becoming the media hub of Britain, MediaCityUK; we love the lights, the glass, the ordered buildings, everything in its place. When we flew out to our Spanish home, however, our whole lifestyle changed, and it would take us no time at all to pick up our alter ego lives. There were wild boars on our mountain, my washing dried in minutes. We could pick lemons and oranges by the roadside. I did not wear heels or pencil skirts. We took it for granted that a fiesta would no doubt be on the horizon, where tomatoes would be thrown, bulls would run, and our neighbours would go to bed from 2pm until 6pm most days.

Many a Saturday in Manchester is spent on Market Street, shopping, perhaps lunch at a smart new bar in Spinningfields (or, sometimes, Wetherspoons...), and then a big shop at Sainsbury's or Tesco. Conversely, many a Saturday when we were in Spain would be spent around Jalon Valley, a half-hour drive from our house. Jalon Valley is also known as Xaló, the Valencian spelling, as well as Vall de Pop, and is made up of the main village of Jalon, along with Alcalalí, Llíber and Parcent. This is the perfect trip, because they appear to have seen sense, and don't close for a four-hour siesta. By 'they' I mean the wine *bodegas*!

One of our favourite moments of last year was, while strolling around the lovely village square, seeing a huge lorryful of green bulbus grapes; another picture postcard moment that we didn't need to capture, as it will always be in our hearts. I cannot comment on the red wine produced in the area, but the white wine is beautifully dry and crisp, while the Moscatel sweet dessert wine is stunning. As one can imagine, bulk-buying is called for, and the thrill of filling up your own five-litre bottles of wine and handing over a five euro note for the pleasure is almost as much fun as drinking the fine nectar!

While I was still in broken ankle mode, as mentioned earlier, Bob took me to one of the *bodegas* to have the necessary 'thrill of the fill', as it were. The *bodega* was so crowded that he wheeled me just inside the entrance to escape the burning sun of the hinterland, and he left me for a few moments while completing his task. I had removed my rather snazzy M&S sun hat and was sitting peacefully watching people slug the free samples when I was approached by a lady who proceeded to lean over me, so close that I could see every cavernous pore. Obviously working on the premise that a person sitting in a wheelchair is not only half-blind, but they must also have lost the faculty of hearing, she shouted, stressing every word, "You have a label in your hair! It says, 'keep away from fire'! I am telling you this because it is making you look VERY stupid!" I thanked her profusely by the only method this short-sighted, deaf, disabled woman could do... with an internationally-understood hand gesture.

Over the years we have learned many things about wine, and one is that it doesn't keep very well in five-litre plastic bottles in our outside metal storeroom. However, the joy of visiting the *bodegas* continues, but these days we tend to buy a more modestly-sized bottle of cava as a treat.

A perfect time to experience Jalon Valley is in late January/early February, when the almond blossoms jostle to show you their pink or white blossom. Most people think that the name Costa Blanca comes from the white sandy beaches of the region, but it is said that the true meaning of 'white coast' comes from the 'sea' of white that covers the valleys and lower mountains at this time of year. It is said that the trees were planted by the Arabs during their five-hundred-year rule. Many of the houses reflect the influences of that time, with their tiny windows with ornate metal grills, and huge wooden doors that look too big for the property.

As well as almonds, there are fields of oranges and olives. The *rastro* market on a Saturday is renowned as a treasure trove for anything from farming implements to second-hand leather goods (the reason why I now own a Bermans leather skirt, bought at a cost of six euros – I wonder how that got there?), trinkets, handbags – something for everyone. A very serendipitous event happened on one of our latter visits to the market. We had taken Hayley to Jalon many times, however, when she was visiting with her fiancé, now hubby, Sean, we decided to show him around. Hayley and Sean had been telling me about a book they had read on their Kindles entitled *Shadow of the Wind* by Carlos Ruiz Zafón. This epic novel had spent two years on the Spanish bestseller list and had been translated into many languages. The story is set in the author's native Barcelona in the years after the Spanish Civil War, and they thought I would enjoy it, but had not been able to find a copy for me. Imagine Hayley's delight when, walking around the market, she spotted a paperback English-language version of the book. Hayley spoke to the lady stallholder who was selling a variety of domestic items, and who had also loved the book, agreeing with Hayley that it was something very special. So, for the princely sum of one euro, paid by Hayley, the book became mine. This might not appear very dramatic, but when I tell you that the essence of the story is about a book, hidden in the heart of Spain within the 'Cemetery of Forgotten Books', then perhaps you will understand why, for me, Hayley's find becomes quite magical. The book did not disappoint, and I kept it until it decided it was time for me to let it go, and for it to move on to a new reader.

Sometimes when we drove away from Jalon, depending on the amount of wine we might have purchased, we would stop for a picnic in Calpe. A beautiful coastal town famed for tourism and fresh fish, Calpe lies at the foot of a huge rock outcrop and national park of Penyal d'lfac. On seeing the rock for the first time in 2005, I immediately named it 'Gorilla's Head', as that was what it reminded me of. It was so big we could spy it from our roof terrace, but then our roof terrace did afford us a 360-degree view of all the beauty that surrounded us. On one occasion, not knowing how busy Calpe could be in July, even intrepid parking-place-finder Bob could not find anywhere, and poor Hayley, turning green with car sickness, had to be let out of the car. We didn't realise that we had dropped her at the famous fresh fish front of Calpe, usually a place our little Piscean would have relished – but sadly on this occasion it just turned her a darker shade of green!

On relaying the story to our friend Lynn, she stuttered, "What? You call yourselves locals now and you tried to park in Calpe – in July!?"

If Bob hadn't had an alcoholic drink, we would sometimes stop for just one glass of wine at one of many *rastros* on the main road about three miles from our house. At first glance, they look like huge second-hand stores with furniture piled high outside but, on closer inspection, one would see a whole life going on inside, comprising many buildings, like old *fincas*, with nooks and crannies, and people with stalls in tiny rooms, or large outside gardened areas. Everything you have ever wanted can be found at these stalls, from second-hand baby clothes, to fishing boats, to crystals. Some stalls are held by amazing artists showcasing their fabulous works, others have old prints that were popular in the 1960s in Woolworths, most likely brought over by expats in the early days. The bar will be in a tiled area and there will be karaoke or flamenco, such a rich tapestry of life all existing cheek-by-jowl.

I remember being shocked and upset to see a stall selling German and SS military uniforms from the second world war; but then on reflection, how could I be? There are many people of German origin who own or rent property in Spain, so how could I judge them then or now?

Talking of apparel, I sometimes wondered at, and envied, the Spanish people on how they look so cool when it is so hot. The weather in the UK before we left for one of our four-day summer breaks to Spain could reach the low 30s but that would be, of course, the norm for Spain. In fact, we would not see a mention of high temperatures in the local Brit papers until the thermometer tipped above 40 degrees and yet, of course, it would take over the headlines when a July day in London would reach the hottest day on record. We Brits don't 'do' the heat well really, do we?

While I sipped my café con leche, seated outside under a huge sun umbrella, I would imagine Meryl Streep's *The Devil Wears Prada* character, the inimitable Miranda Priestly, self-combusting if any female dared walk into her office in flip-flops and a polyester maxi dress. Or white knee-length nylon leggings and a boho kaftan. She would throw a withering stare at the line "this look takes me from the office to cocktails"!

While on the sartorial subject, I would often muse as to why, for the last few years or so, women had bought their men folk, or had allowed them to wear, shorts that imitated recycled tea cloths? In fairness, there are so many white and grey checked shorts in the shops that it can be difficult for the boys to find anything else during their five-minute 'parachute drop shop' for summer clothes, bless 'em.

For many, myself included, the question remains to this day – what does one wear to a business meeting on a hot day in the UK? 'Effortless summer office chic' provided by our magazine fashion gurus is all well and good, but the model has been photographed in an airconditioned studio, or outside with water mist fans surrounding her – not trying to catch the number 9 bus to work, or having to breathe in one last molecule of air before joining the tube scrum. So, when the fashion gurus finally understand that many of us women like a cool dress with a little sleeve because many of us HATE OUR ARMS, then perhaps we can at last discard the cardigan we keep in the office for when we crawl in from the commute to work, only to be slapped hard by our friend, the welcome blast of aircon – a friendship which turns to enemy proportions when our feet turn to ice around 10.50am?

So, my Bob and I would fly off to our other life in Spain, where we would be told nonchalantly by our neighbours that the weather had reached 45 degrees again, and the only complaint about it would be that their gardens, which mostly comprised of rustica soil, had again suffered. The older women carried fans, and the younger women hadn't got a bead of sweat upon their dusky brows. The businesswomen in town appeared to prefer a black shift dress or white blouse and black or navy skirt and no tights, no hairy legs, and with vertiginous stilettos. It was not then, and is still not now, fair!

Chapter 14:

Coronation Street Square & Lunch with Joyce Temple Savage

Whenever my Bob and I are on our travels across the world, it is a given that we will be asked where we come from. Our reply, "Manchester", always initiates the same response - "Ahhh! Manchester United and Coronation Street!"

It therefore should not have been a surprise to me when, through two friends we had met in Spain, I was asked if I could ask the Coronation Street 'people' if the then Mayor of Benidorm could name a square in the town after the famous street, loved by so many. Thus, Operation Coronation Street Square was born. Never one to refuse a challenge, I interceded between the then Mayor of Benidorm, Señor Vicente Perez Devesa and ITV's legal department.

So it was that in September of 2005, Bob, the two friends and I found ourselves in the Mayor's office at Benidorm Town Hall, an exceedingly modern building in the centre of town.

We were graciously received and, together with an interpreter (it was our first year of learning Spanish) we were introduced and exchanged handshakes, many photos were taken, and I received a lovely book about Benidorm, signed by the Mayor. We truly believed the moment was over and as we followed the Mayor and his assistants, we thought we were being shown out through the front door. As the huge double doors open, we realised very quickly, that we were actually the main event of a huge press conference. As I was shown to the imposing dais, I was relieved to see the interpreter arrive to my rescue. The Mayor gave a speech and I was asked to give my own, impromptu, speech, while both were simultaneously interpreted, and flash bulbs aplenty sparked across the lecture theatre. Bob later likened the experience to watching the top three Grand Prix Drivers being interviewed following a race!

The Mayor stood, I stood, we shook hands and he went to leave. I followed, but no – I was ushered back into the room to be interviewed by various members of the press, none of whom spoke English. My Spanish was appalling at that time, and the wonderful interpreter had also left the room.

It was no surprise that over the course of the following days, the event was in many national, local papers, both in Spain and in the UK. In some papers I was exalted to leader of all sorts of organisations but all comments on the initiative were very favourable.

I was relieved that history had not repeated itself as, a few years prior, I was delighted to be asked to represent the then-Mayor of Stockport on a goodwill visit to Torremolinos in southern Spain, where a new statue had been erected to the *entente cordiale* of both towns. At the time, I was honoured to be working on a charity initiative with the, now late, Duke of Westminster. It was reported in their local Torremolinos newspaper the following week that I was representing the Duke of Wellington! Well, I was having a bad hair day and was very tired.

Back to Benidorm 2005. Obviously, there are many things that Mayors have to do during their tenure and as other initiatives took precedence, the actual naming of Coronation Street Square never happened. Other Mayors have since been in office and the naming of Coronation Street Square was forgotten. We noticed in 2017 that the intended area had been built upon, and a hotel stands in its place.

Benidorm is popular with so many people right across Europe, so more beds available so that more people can visit and enjoy all the town has to offer seems most appropriate. There are few people in Britain who do not know of the hit TV series, 'Benidorm.' Bob and I were delighted when our good friend, actress, Sherrie Hewson announced in 2012 that she was joining the cast of 'Benidorm' then to be in its 5th series. I remember warning her that as she would start filming in March, when the skies were blue and the sun shined, that in fact from 3pm in the afternoon it turned blooming cold. We noticed that she had heeded our words and no doubt those of her co-stars as when we met her for a coffee near Poniente Beach, she was wearing sunglasses and was swathed in her fake fur. It also helped, I thought for her privacy too. Soon Sherrie, with her perfect comic timing, was a regular on the programme and became a firm favourite with the viewers. On one occasion we had our lovely mutual friend, Elaine, staying with us, so we had all agreed to meet up on a sunny day in Albir for Sunday lunch. In the gorgeous weather the fake fur had gone and Sherrie, alongside her makeup artist friend, were soon beeping us to gain our attention as they drove up in their open top car. After the usual excitement of us all seeing each other, Sherrie told me that she wanted us to show her a typical Spanish Sunday lunch. I explained to Sherrie that whilst we could find that on Tapas Alley (Calle de Tapas) in Benidorm, where the whole street has the most tapas bars/restaurants – an area she knew well, sadly, in the outer quieter town, most families ate together at their relatives (all terrified of letting down mama and her paella!) We also loved how, in the summer months, on the quieter beaches that we had learned how to find, the locals would arrive with trestle tables, folding chairs and garden marquees and set up their family feasts -which always meant no less than 15 people having a great Sunday. After we had driven around and around and around even Sherrie gave in and so it was that we ended up having our authentic Spanish Sunday lunch in a Japanese restaurant.

Chapter 15

Sold!

As the months turned into years and still no buyers, we wondered when the 'right' time would come. And happen it did – as suspected, in the most serendipitous way.

While celebrating New Year 2016 in Spain with Hayley and her lovely Sean, whom we love dearly, Hayley noticed a small sign on the wall of a neighbouring house. It was an estate agent's sign, advertising a small number of houses featured in a glass box. Hayley took a picture with her phone and when we next had internet, we perused the estate agent's website. "This is it!" we all shouted in unison. Surely, we all agreed, an immediately local estate agent must attract people who want to live in the area!

On our return to England, I sent the agency an email, and received a reply from a lady called Stephanie. We agreed to meet for a coffee at the only bar on the urbanisation the next time we were in Spain, which was to be early April, and we were to bring a set of keys for her.

We gleaned that Stephanie was from Belgium. But other than this snippet of information, we had no idea what she looked like. But since the bar was small, we thought we wouldn't have a problem identifying her. Oh dear, how wrong we were!

As we didn't frequent the bar, we didn't know any of its regulars either. When we walked in, there was only one male and female couple in there, who smiled and nodded, and we smiled back. "Hello," said the man, "come and sit!" Presuming this was Stephanie and her husband, and surprised that their English accents were so good, we walked over and duly shook hands with the man and his female companion, who stood up and embraced us. Bob shot me a bewildered look, as we had presumed they would be a little more formal. The couple's glasses were full, and Bob asked them in a perfunctory manner if they would care for anything else while he ordered our coffees. Another look was shot at me from Bob as they both shouted "beer!"

Eventually seated with our drinks, we began to talk about houses on the estate and, in particular, their house, and how we would love it as they had a jacuzzi on the roof. I decided it was time that the conversation was brought back to OUR house and so said to the man, "We have seen your website and we were impressed. We've brought an extra set of our house keys with us!" Bob then proceeded to put the keys in the middle of the table. The man's demeanour became very animated and he said how pleased he was I liked the website. Fortunately, at that very moment, a voice from behind us said, "Ummm, Mr and Mrs Carter? May we discuss your property now?" Bob and I must have looked guilty, bewildered, and possibly a mixture of both. We both just stared at the new couple standing by us, dressed in office attire. We hastily composed ourselves and, just as hastily, moved to a different table with just a quick nod to whomever we had just spent the last fifteen minutes with.

We really liked Stephanie and her husband and felt they would be the ones to procure us a sale on our casa. After a few false starts with some prospective buyers, a year or so after our first meeting, we received The Call from Stephanie, the call we had waited so long for... and we should have known that, there in the background, our old friend Bill would have something to do with it, too! All we knew was, we had a sale!

As we now knew, nothing moves quickly in Spain, and it was almost Christmas before we signed on the dotted line. Our lovely friend Pete, still known to us as 'Bill's Pete', was our Power of Attorney and witness as we visited the Notary for the last time.

Our other lovely friend Lynne and her friend helped us to strip the house as the new buyers didn't want anything left in.

Bob and I kept only a very small amount of our personal items to take back to England. In the fourteen years we had enjoyed our casa, the airlines had changed their policies, and there was no way I would now be able to transport cupboards in a suitcase for just the cost of buying a ticket home. We didn't care; this chapter of our dream was complete, and it was time to move on. As expected, we would wait at least another year to receive any local or regional tax rebates and the like that were owed to us. At least the power of the internet meant we would be able to keep in touch with our dear friends.

Another year went by and we received the news from our friends that, yes! A supermarket had finally opened on urbanisation! Fifteen years too late for us but, never mind, we had no regrets.

And what of us, you ask? Since then, we have completed a three-thousand-kilometre *adiós* tour of Spain, visiting areas of this vast, mainly unspoiled, country of multi-contrasting vistas, of plains and mountains, that we had not already seen, visited or climbed. We continue to visit Spain at least once a year, as Spain is an old friend to us now. *¡Gracias España!*

We have decided that, fifteen years later than originally planned, France is definitely the next country for us, however... this time, we will not buy a property, we will rent!

Acknowledgement

With grateful thanks to Bill Abraham for finding us our Casa de Suenos and standing by us!

Pete Johnson for not killing Bill - on so many occasions- and our thanks to both gentlemen for helping us in so many ways, including the sale of our property.

Lyn Schofield-Keane, author in her own right *Absent Minders* and to whom I will always give my thanks for urging me to carry on and "write it down!" Thanks for cakes and for New Year's Day around the fire.

To Hayley Smith MA ACIL for proofreading this book.
Any mistakes are because the author meddled post proofreading - sorry Hayley!
hslinguist.wixsite.com/hslinguist

Printed in Poland
by Amazon Fulfillment
Poland Sp. z o.o., Wrocław

58096691R00076